Long Life Expectations for Old Age

We're wrong to be afraid of old age, says Dr Magnus Pyke, in this heartening and honest book about what being elderly means today. Taking advantage of all the achievements of modern science, one can reasonably expect a further twenty years of life after retirement, and the enjoyment of good health for the greater part of that time. The elderly, asserts Dr Pyke, can now profoundly influence both their own future and the future development of our society.

Dr Magnus Pyke, known to millions of television-viewers for his lively contributions to programmes on science, education and matters of general interest, has written *Long Life* under the auspices of the British Association for the Advancement of Science, of which he is a former Secretary and Chairman of Council. The book springs from the work of the Committee on Aging, a distinguished study-group set up by the BA in 1974, and the foreword is by Dr W. F. Bodmer and Professor Sir Ferguson Anderson, who were respectively Chairman and Vice-Chairman of the committee at the time of its formation.

Dr Pyke's book is encouraging, sympathetic and humorous. He focuses on the everyday life of the aged; on practical problems and how they can be overcome; and, most important, on ways in which we can enjoy more fully this particular phase of our long life.

Dr Magnus Pyke

Long Life

Expectations for Old Age

J M Dent & Sons Ltd London Toronto Melbourne

First published 1980
© Dr Magnus Pyke 1980

Printed in Great Britain by
Biddles Ltd, Guildford, Surrey
for J. M. Dent & Sons Ltd
Aldine House, 33 Welbeck Street, London
This book is set in 11/13pt VIP Plantin
by Trident Graphics Limited, Reigate, Surrey

British Library Cataloguing in Publication Data
Pyke, Magnus
Expectations for old age
1 Old age
I Title
301.43'5   HQ1061

ISBN 0–460–04481–8
ISBN 0–460–02211–3 Pbk

Contents

Foreword

The origins of this book come from a series of meetings of the Committee for Social Concern and Biological Advances of the British Association for the Advancement of Science. The authors of this foreword were respectively Chairman and Vice-chairman of this committee while the author of the book, Dr Magnus Pyke, was Secretary of the BA during the committee's formative stages. Our British Association Group started originally in 1971 with generous funding from the Leverhulme Trust Fund and was concerned with discussion of the problems connected with advances in genetics and related areas. These earlier discussions culminated in a book called *Our Future Inheritance: Choice or Chance?* by Alun Jones and Walter Bodmer. The problems of aging, medical and social, are among the greatest challenges of our time and thus were a most appropriate choice for the next stage of discussion of the Committee on Social Concern and Biological Advances. At the end of 1974, therefore, we effectively became the BA Committee on Aging and during the last five years have met frequently and had help from a great many people with expert knowledge in various aspects of aging.

Now that in the UK and most modern industrialized societies the birth rate has declined to match the low death rate achieved as a result of improved hygiene, nutrition and medical care, the age structure of the population, that is the proportions of people of different ages, has altered dramatically. In a rapidly expanding population there are many young and relatively few older people. Today there is not much difference in the proportions of people at different ages, which means that the proportion of the population which is made up of older people is very much increased. In Britain now the proportion of the population over the age of sixty-five is about 14 per cent, while about 6 per cent are over seventy-five, and these proportions will not change very much during the next twenty to thirty years. The proportion of the very old, say those over eighty-five, will still, of course, change and increase as our ability to deal with the diseases of old people increases. By the year 2000 the proportion of people over eighty-five years of age will probably have increased by more than 50 per cent, although they will then still constitute less than 10 per cent of those over the age of sixty-five. But the significant effect of achieving a stable situation such as we now have in Britain, with a low birth rate and a low death rate, is not so much this increase in the number of very old people and the attendant medical and social problems, it is rather the complete change in the age structure, the fact that a greater proportion of the population than ever before is made up of old people. Herein lies a major problem which our society is only now beginning to face. The social and medical problems of the over-sixty-fives are enormous and quite inadequately appreciated. A large proportion of our medical care goes to them and their medical problems may often be different from and more complex than those of the younger sections of the population. Poverty, housing and other social problems are also accentuated at the present time with increasing age. But does this have to be the case? Thought must be given, in our modern industrialized societies, to changes in retirement policy and to the pro-vision of more opportunities for continuing work and for changing one's occupation – at any age, but especially from middle age onwards.

A great increase in the number of people aged over eighty is something which will also be seen in underdeveloped countries in the next twenty-five years. The immense problems it will pose will be exacerbated by the movement of rural populations to urban areas, by the breaking up of tribal groups with a subsequent loss of community spirit, and by the loosening of family ties through emigration. We must all be prepared to face the problems of the elderly in this wider context.

In the various meetings of our Aging Committee we have discussed a wide range of issues, and in particular we have had four productive and stimulating weekend meetings at Cumberland Lodge to which colleagues have come giving us their precious weekend time, and which have formed the basis for an extensive series of notes. We have also arranged symposia and contributed to others. Throughout all these discussions Dr Magnus Pyke has been an active member of the group, and about two years ago we suggested to him that perhaps he would be the right person to write a book which would be the aging 'successor' to our previous publication. This book is, then, the result of that suggestion and is based to a considerable extent on the material our committee has produced and the many contacts we have made with people in the aging field. Special thanks are due to Professor Tom Arie (Sherwood Hospital, Nottingham), Dr F. I. Caird (Southern General Hospital, Glasgow), Professor Canon G. F. Dunstan (King's College, London), Dr Anne McLaren, FRS (MRC Mammalian Development Unit, University College, London), Mr Edward Walton (formerly Link Opportunity Study), Dame Margaret Miles, DBE and Mrs Ursula Laver, rapporteur to the BA Committee on Aging.

The book however, is not just a record of our deliberations or a summary of the views of the members of the committee. Dr Magnus Pyke, in his own fascinating way, gives a highly sympathetic and personal account which we believe should appeal to a wide audience. He provides much needed encouragement for the elderly, and his discussion of many of their problems will, we hope, make many people conscious of the need for a change in our attitude and approach to them. We hope, too, that this book will bring home the fact that the place the elderly will hold in tomorrow's society is a question of vital importance, not only for them but for the whole of the community.

Dr W. F. Bodmer FRS
Director of Research, Imperial Cancer Research Fund
Laboratories

Professor Sir Ferguson Anderson OBE
Cargill Professor of Geriatric Medicine, University of
Glasgow

1979

1 Rewards at Any Age

Alice in Wonderland may have been written for children but it contains a lot of sound sense for grown-up people as well. And among such grown-up citizens, old people living in our present technological age can learn a lesson of special importance from the attitude of that admirable old stick, Father William.

'You are old, Father William,' the young man said,
'And your hair has become very white;
And yet you incessantly stand on your head –
Do you think, at your age, it is right?'

Here we have, in 1865 when the book was written, just as we do today, the young man, a sociological research worker, no doubt, with his clipboard and questionnaire, collecting data on the behaviour of the elderly, and doing so with highly praiseworthy intentions. Then comes the answer which, like the question, has much to tell us for our own benefit today.

'In my youth,' Father William replied to his son,
'I feared it might injure the brain,

(And, no doubt, at that time he gave up smoking, taking sugar in his tea and eating fatty acids, besides getting a prescription from his doctor for tranquillizers)

But now that I'm perfectly sure I have none;
Why I do it again and again.'

The proposition is not, of course, that elderly people

1

should stand on their heads. What they, and the rest of us, should do, however, is to take note both of the lessons of history and of common sense, and of the newer knowledge of science as well, which teach us to recognize elderly people as citizens as valuable, useful, human and versatile within the ambit of *their* faculties as are any other group within the community. Just as people in their thirties are to be found writing books, running businesses, working in factories and offices, taking part in round-Britain bicycle races or earning their living as deep-sea trawlermen, and people in their twenties have occupations ranging from heavyweight boxing to the writing of poetry, so, too, can elderly people properly engage themselves in as wide a variety of activities.

As the saying goes, there are horses for courses. An experienced trainer knows perfectly well that a colt with a reputation for sprinting is unlikely to do well in a race over a mile and a half on heavy going. An expert in veterinary science can explain in some detail why this is so, but, although it may be satisfying to understand this and, indeed, it may be useful to do so, it adds little, for the most part, to what the trainer already knew, nor would it help an intellectual horse who had the intuition (as has a man) to be aware of its own capacity. Similarly, while a gerontologist, that is, an expert in the science of aging, can explain the biochemical differences between, say, a schoolchild, a student full of healthy revolt, a middle-aged factory supervisor and the Archbishop of Canterbury, any sensible person is aware that there are bodily differences and that an elderly person is unlikely to be seen hop-skipping and jumping along the road like a six-year-old child. It sometimes happens, however, that common sense does not hold sway when people think about one particular slice of life – old age. Not only does the community as a whole, with the best will in the world, sometimes fail to understand what it is to be elderly, but those who themselves are elderly, or on the verge of being so, can hold uninformed and unscientific ideas on the subject as well.

The first point which it is the purpose of this chapter to make is that each stage in life possesses its own peculiar advantages and provides its own special rewards, just as it has its particular hardships and troubles. All that modern scientific understanding can do is to point out some of the reasons why this is so. We all know that life extends as a continuous thread from birth to death. The colour and texture of the thread changes as life goes on. Science describes what some of the changes are; it cannot supply a meaningful specification distinguishing the chemistry of an active, useful, happy person as life goes by. There are happy babies and miserable ones. Childhood, too, can be a happy time (that is *its* reward) but it can also be a period of fear and uncertainty, paralysing shyness and dreadful nightmares. The sentimental song sighs for the time 'when you and I were seventeen'. Our physique and biochemistry are then near or at their peak of efficiency. The rewards at this period of life are great indeed. All the world, as the song goes on to say, is new. Just the same, adolescence can also be a time of searing doubts, of self-blame, of dreadful pangs of unrequited love, of fears of damnation and of apprehensions for the future. There is a peak, at this time, in the statistics of suicide.

What does it profit a young man or woman to know that, having passed through the period as a child when he or she could absorb calcium at such a rate that the entire calcium content of the skeleton was replaced in about two years, now that he or she is ready to become the heavyweight boxing champion of the world (not that many women go in for boxing), or an Olympic gold medalist, it takes the healthiest adult ten to twelve years to acquire a new skeleton's-worth of calcium? And if a middle-aged man, rising rapidly in the world's esteem – for that is one of the rewards of being forty-five – yet

worried by his wife's extravagance, his children's irres-
ponsibility and the monthly payments on the car – which
are some of the penalties – gives little thought to the fact
that, far from being able to replace his calcium any more,
the amount he carries in his skull and bones is beginning to dwindle, why should elderly people worry either
because of the fact that, just as in infancy the calcium in
their bones builds up, in later life it flows away again?
Most people live and die without knowing this or suffering any disability from its happening. And since few
people in their seventies and eighties *want* to play rugby
football, it is hardly worth going much out of one's way
to tell those who do why it is physiologically undesirable
to expose their less calcified thigh bones to the strain.

Scientific study can provide a great deal of detailed
information to explain why it is that the composition of
the human body and the efficiency with which it functions are different at different times of life. It is only *one*
part of science, however, that concerns itself with observ-
ing, for example, that, over the average of a 'cohort' of
individuals, ten-year-old boys could do less work, as
measured by turning a handle or gripping with their
'dominant' hand, than men of twenty who, in turn, were
less strong than men of thirty; while groups of men aged
fifty, sixty and seventy were progressively less muscular.
So far as science depends on the collection of accurate
information about what goes on in the natural universe,
it can also bear witness to the fact that many highly
effective, lively and creative people can continue as such
through the seventh, eighth and even ninth decades of
life. A man's degree of muscular strength has little bearing on his determination to get work done, and experience in shipwrecks – to take a rather extreme example –
has often shown that it is less muscular castaways who
survive when their more powerful companions lose hope.
Nor does it follow, particularly in this age of automation,
fork-lift trucks and mammoth earth-moving machinery,

that because a man at seventy may only be as physically strong as he was sixty years before when he was ten, that he is not up to a job on a building site or in a shipyard if he wants to work in one or the other. And it has repeatedly been shown that it is the young men with quick reaction times, keen eyesight and trained physique who are most likely to be involved in road accidents when driving a car, whereas elderly men, whose physiology will have been modified by time but whose judgment has been ripened by experience, are the safest drivers.

As our understanding of the detailed physiological changes which take place throughout life increases, there is a growing tendency for these changes to be described in the most technical terms. But, after all, to talk about the more rapid rate at which young men and women are capable of burning up the glucose in their blood stream during the course of violent exercise is merely to repeat in more technical detail the well recognized rise and fall in athletic performance as each decade succeeds the one before. Our understanding of one among several of the time changes which occur as life progresses can, however, be of direct *practical* value to the elderly. Throughout our days we are all of us mostly water; but it has been found that if it be assumed that the amount of water in the bodies of young adults is given the arbitrary figure of 100, the amount present in people of sixty is, on average, 90, while that present at the age of eighty is about 80. While this is a normal change, it has been observed that the sense of thirst of some perfectly healthy and effective old people can become blunted and that in consequence they drink less fluid than they need. The upshot is that they become dehydrated without knowing it. How curious it would be if the predeliction of our ancestors for 'taking the waters' – at Bath, Harrogate, Baden Baden and a dozen other hydropathic centres – which was once held in some esteem by the medical faculty, should become once again justified on scientific evidence fifty years or more after it had been abandoned as orthodox medical treatment. But perhaps, after all, one or two extra glasses of water during the day's normal activities would answer the purpose just as well.

The organ which science has subjected to the closest scrutiny of all is the brain. When a human being has reached the age of twenty-five the brain is probably at its maximum size, though oddly enough its capacity is greatest when there is least in it – during the first years of life; for, of course, it is important that it is at its most receptive in these early years. It is also to be remembered that the ability of the brain to store information is of little significance; its power to retain, recall and combine thoughts is so great that in all probability the amount of stored information which is ever brought into use is only a small fraction of the whole. This holds equally for children, for young adults, for the middle-aged and for the old whose brains, like their muscles, have decreased in size. It is interesting to observe how the function of the brain becomes modified so as to provide both the penalties and rewards attaching to the human condition at different ages. In childhood, the brain, not functioning as fully as it will later, provides rewards for its owner as, stage by stage, it apprehends the wonders of the world. On the other hand, few things are the source of more acute misery than the unformed mind of a child set to grapple with a lesson in reading which is too difficult. The big-minded students in their early twenties reap the reward of knowing that at their age are conceived many of the seminal ideas which will lead, for the most gifted and committed, to the discoveries on which they will work for the rest of their lives. The penalty for people in this group is in the discovery, which anyone with some degree of insight cannot avoid making, that their power of retention – then at its peak – and their intellectual ability are less, sometimes much less, than those of others in whose eyes they would dearly love to be seen to excel. This may come as a heavy blow.

For the elderly, the mature mind, smaller than it once was and with fewer cells but – as the track record of Paderewski, Kenyatta, Bertrand Russell and Chevreul (a French chemist who went on making discoveries until he was a hundred) shows – none the worse for that, provides many rewards for its fortunate owner. It has a store of past experiences and acquired knowledge on which it can draw. It is the better able to reject many of the unreasonable, misguided and downright erroneous novelties which can deflect the minds of the young and, memory for new things being less retentive, the older person may discard much of the ephemora with which the popular consciousness is too often cluttered. Compared with these rewards, the penalties are slight. Not to be able to carry a seven-figure telephone number across the room is a minor handicap in a world where telephone directories are plentiful. Nor did my grandmother, a forceful old lady to the end, suffer much disadvantage in remembering me by my father's name when, in her memory, she saw his qualities revived again in me.

History is crowded with accounts of the rewards which come to the elderly from the physiological changes which lend the particular quality to their brains. In our own time, Picasso, Chairman Mao, Sir Adrian Boult, Arthur Askey, and Dame Hariet Chick (a distinguished biochemist who was still addressing learned meetings in her hundredth year) represent a variety of achievement. In this context, the scientific observation that the weight of the mean (that is 'average') brain is 1,400 grams at the age of twenty and has diminished to 1,200 grams by the age of eighty, though interesting, no doubt, is unimportant. It is not how many grams-worth of brain men and women have in their craniums that matters but what their brains have been trained to do. There is, however, at least one intellectual faculty on which scientific study can make useful comment. It appears that the capacity to stand erect on two feet, one of the basic characteristics of the human being, is not built-in but – as any baby might be expected to know – something which has to be laboriously learned and remembered. In this respect, people are less accomplished than birds. Birds, like people, stand on two legs. Unlike human beings, however, birds do not have to learn to stand but are able to keep themselves erect as soon as they step out of their shells. There are even those possessing – without learning – so remarkable a degree of postural control that they are able to sleep standing on *one* leg. Human beings, on the other hand, find it necessary to spend a considerable amount of time learning – and practising what they have learnt – before they are able to stand up without falling. The erect stance, it can now be recognized, is a skill whose execution is dependent on a store of memories laid down during the intellectual process of learning. A tennis player, while running at full stretch diagonally across the court in one direction, can hit a tennis ball coming towards him in a different direction so that it flies back at an angle so finely judged that it exactly clips a selected portion of the opposite base line – but he can only do so after learning and practice which permit him to carry out instantaneously, albeit unconsciously, a complicated series of calculations which must be translated into a series of equally intricate neural and muscular responses. The same holds for the only slightly less complex operation of balancing oneself erect.

A series of scientific studies was carried out about ten years ago to assess the ability of people to stand without wobbling at the different stages of life. Between the ages of six and nine, children can of course stand erect but, when the measurements are carefully made, it can be shown that their control mechanism is not particularly good and they wobble as they stand. Between ten and fourteen, their performance is better but not good. Only by the age of sixteen have they learnt the trick. This they retain up to about fifty. Thereafter – so it is found – the learned reactions slip away and by the time they are eighty their skill is about the same as it was when they were nine. This is interesting to know although, in the common-sense world of everyday, it has long been known. Nor is it very much of a penalty to be asked to pay for the rewards of seniority. It merely implies that there is a good physiological reason for an elderly man or woman to use a walking-stick.

People of one age-group – the forty-year-olds, let us say – looking at those in their twenties, or at those in their teens, frequently remember the rewards and forget the penalties of these times. 'School days', they may say – having long ago left the schoolroom themselves – 'are the happiest days of your life'. This is by no means self-evident. Even if we leave aside the social disadvantages of being bullied, there are physiological reasons why the young are not necessarily to be envied. Scientific assessment has it that when we are young we possess on average 245 taste buds on our tongues; when we are old, the average has fallen to 90. This need not be a matter for regret. It is the young who suffer from the *disgusting* taste of stewed rhubarb and who *hate* the fat on mutton chops with a degree of distaste which makes the eating of it torture to them. An older group within the community can look back with enjoyment at the time they first savoured – with the surprised (and not always pleasurable) acuteness of youth – an oyster or a plate of mulligatawny soup and take a delight, greater in retrospect than it ever was in reality, in recalling that cake mother used to bake. What matter if they know now that mother had been a terrible cook, they loved *her* to the end.

Life is a continual process of change. To a philosophical mind, it is fruitless to try to rank its various stages in order of their agreeability, or importance, or usefulness. Happiness can come at any age. Heroic deeds that illuminate human history can be done by old men and women as well as by young ones. Christ made his contribution and died in his thirties. Pope John set a standard for Christianity in his eighties. Although, decade by decade, people's skin loses its elasticity, the colour of their hair changes to grey, their visual acuity decreases and their field of vision becomes more restricted, it verges on the frivolous to imply that because these changes occur the capacity of an elderly person to contribute to what is valuable in the world – or to savour the delights of living – is any the less. A man or woman does not dwindle as such because he or she wears glasses (though ophthalmological science has now, of course, provided the alternative of contact lenses, for those who want to bother with them). Nelson – or for that matter, Moshe Dayan – did not allow the loss of an eye to hamper his active and noble participation in the affairs of his country.

One of the changes which affects the eyes of the elderly as time goes by, and might seem to those of a reflective temperament to be of some philosophical significance, is that the lens of the eye tends to become less flexible than it was and this causes the long-sightedness which often makes it necessary for elderly people to wear spectacles for reading. Sometimes, however, the combination of ocular changes will cause the refractive index of the less flexible lens to alter in such a way as to counterbalance the impairment of accommodation. When this happens, after years of being able to read the newspaper only with glasses, an elderly person finds, to his surprise, that he can do so again without them. Ophthalmologists have called this phenomenon 'second sight'. But with or without glasses, sensible elderly people will know that it is the wisdom they have gained through experience which will best enable them to apprehend what is going on in the world.

Let me not denigrate the value of scientific study of the changes that mark the progression of life. By understanding, a man or woman can be saved from attempting activities beyond his or her capabilities: most people have enough sense to stop playing rugby football at forty and most communities have enough wit to prevent the young motor-cycling before the age of sixteen. What science can tell is interesting in its own right. It is also useful. We know that hearing is at its most sensitive at the age of about twenty and that thereafter the nerve cells by which sound is apprehended begin to lose their 'edge'; also that the reception of high notes is blunted more than that of low notes. Such knowledge is useful now that progress in communications and in electronic miniaturization makes it possible to provide hearing aids for those who feel that they need to interpret more of the ambient cacophony than their unaided ears can manage. Sir Adrian Boult, it is interesting to note, celebrated his twentieth birthday seventy years ago – would anyone consider him unfit to conduct the orchestra at the Albert Hall?

Old Father William is described in the poem as standing on his head, balancing an eel on the end of his nose, finishing the goose with the bones and the beak, and turning a back somersault in at the door. This can be taken as a parable implying that, as in any of the other periods of life, there are many lively activities which can appropriately be undertaken in old age. Perhaps today there are some peculiar difficulties facing anyone in search of a purpose in life. Once upon a time, the forces of nature posed so palpable a threat that it clearly needed all a man's strength and fortitude to stand up to the troubles and dangers with which he was confronted. When the outcome of every voyage was in doubt, the life of one's wife in childbirth and one's children in infancy hanging on a thread, and the stability of one's livelihood in constant danger from civil disorganization, it was easy to recognize a code of values to which a virtuous man could adhere to guide himself through the vicissitudes and uncertainty of life. Science, in popular acceptance, has changed all that. Wives and children do not die; air-traffic controllers assure the safe (if not always punctual) arrival after every journey; and all over the world measures are taken to ensure the maintenance of factory hygiene, protection from unfair dismissal, and appropriately rewarded employment.

If it be objected that what I have written is exaggeration, it does, at least, show the direction which progress is taking. Aldous Huxley's satire, *Brave New World*, written half a century ago, has proved itself to be a reflection of reality. Science, and the technology developed from it, have provided a safe life richly endowed with sophisticated material possessions. The motives for fortitude and struggle having been thus diminished, pleasure has come to be regarded as the chief good. And to experience pleasure one must, it seems, possess such material adjuncts as a 'hi-fi music centre' and indulge frequently in sexual activity. People have always been attracted to sex, but today the backing of what otherwise serious-minded people have taken to be scientific argument has been mobilized to give respectability to what in any other age would have been recognized as vulgar pandering to the sexual appetite – we, from the oldest to the youngest, are expected to savour it. The age of sexual maturity in women, as indicated by the onset of the menstrual cycle, is influenced by a number of factors including the level of nutrition. In 1860, during the Industrial Revolution, when many of the children in the societies which were industrializing were under-fed, the average age of puberty in girls was sixteen and a half. By 1900, the age had fallen to fifteen; by 1920, puberty occurred on average at fourteen and a half; and by 1960, it was down to thirteen. But though scientific assessment may show us this trend, the deep feelings of sensitive people, the truths of the highest human emotion as expressed in poetry and literature and the bitter records of our own time, all bear

witness to the fact that human happiness and the quality
of life are diminished rather than enhanced by unre-
stricted preoccupation with the technical manifestations
of eroticism as a scientific exercise. The lover 'sighing
like a furnace', as Shakespeare puts it, 'with a woeful
ballad made to his mistress' eyebrow', powerfully expre-
sses an appropriate human reaction to the biological
attainment of full sexual efficiency or, in the terms used
by Bernard Shaw, the response of two individuals to the
'life force'.

Within a period of thirty to thirty-five years, the
reproductive life of most women is over when, at the age
of forty-five or fifty, they reach the menopause. Yet even
though this signals the end of one phase of life and the
start of another, it in no way marks the cessation of love
and affection. Love between two people can be experienced at any stage of life and bring with it all the rewards
and anxieties which any deep relationship involves. In
healthy men, sexual potency continues from the time of
puberty virtually up to the end of life. Lawyers have long
experience of the world behind them when, in dealing
with wills dividing an estate between each of the
offspring of a putative testator, they refuse to make the
division until the said testator is finally dead. This legal
assumption, that no man, however old can be deemed
incapable of fathering a child – as distinct from women,
whose childbearing time comes to an identifiable end –
is a fair reflection of physiological truth. Yet let it be said
that, for men and women of all ages, not only the elderly,
the teasing attention, the incessant talk and the vulgar
prying into the detailed manifestations of sexual performance bring, not only the repetitive titilation which is
particularly characteristic of the current times, but
nagging anxiety that perhaps the performer is doing it
wrong and, where the performance is so often repeated
without the essential justification of love and respect, the
sadness of hollow disappointment and frustration. There

are continent bachelors of all ages just as there are chaste spinsters whose contribution to their community is as great as anybody else's. In married life when the 'life force' has had its way and sex becomes less important, the partners do not suddenly become less happy or less useful members of society; and there is no reason why they should not remain as devoted to each other and as fulfilled in their marriage as they ever were.

Father William of the poem was undoubtedly an eccentric old gentleman. Perhaps, however, we are not meant to take too seriously the particular occupations in which he was reported to indulge. The important lesson his attitude teaches is that those extra twenty or thirty years which science has given to so many of us, in this century can be used for all kinds of endeavour. There are a number of things wrong with the way our present society organizes things for these valuable years, and many elderly people themselves are pretty silly in the role they accept for this valuable portion of their life. On the other hand, the current system could be made the basis for something quite remarkable. But before discussing this, let me first outline some of the dramatic advances in biological science which give promise that some of the disabilities which currently bedevil people's later years could quite rapidly be overcome.

2 Scientific Promise

It is a surprising thing in this scientific age, when it is widely believed that every disease and ill to which man was once subject can be avoided by scientific means, that, alone within the community, elderly people accept as inevitable a number of disabilities which can in fact be avoided. Nor is the widespread apprehension of disaster and decay in old age necessarily justified. Very many of the more insidious and melancholy conditions which can afflict the elderly, affect only a small minority of them. It is mistaken, therefore, for the majority to resign themselves to uselessness, idleness and poverty in the belief that, even though they may be in good order at the time when they opt out of meaningful activity, they are justified in doing so because breakdown and incompetence must be imminent. It would be equally rational to liquidate all the dogs in the United Kingdom for fear that rabies might break out among them, regardless of the fact that, firstly, the preventive measures to avoid its occurrence have been strikingly successful over the last fifty years and, secondly, even in Western Europe where rabies is endemic, the chances of dying of rabies are approximately equal to those of being struck by lightning, an eventuality which is never permitted to serve as an excuse for inaction.

Even though the scientific study of diseases and disabilities of the elderly has been neglected, the amount of new knowledge which has been collected is, as I shall show, formidable. It is sufficiently formidable, indeed, to

15

justify a radical change, not only in the way society regards the capabilities and usefulness of the elderly, but also in the way the elderly assess themselves. There is poetic justice in scientific knowledge now being applied to the maintenance of this significant group within the community since its present size and importance is due to the effectiveness with which science has been applied to the diseases of the young. The numbers and – one would reasonably argue – the corresponding political power – of the elderly, making their health and vigour a matter of such importance for society, have come upon our industrialized societies suddenly and, it would seem, have taken us by surprise. In Holland, to take a convenient example, there were in 1899 60,000 elderly people in every million. In 1910 the proportion was much the same, and in 1920 it was little different. In 1930 the number was only 62,000 in each million. Then things began to happen. By 1940 in each million those in their sixties and older amounted to 70,000; by 1950, to 90,000; and by 1960, to 100,000. The situation then stabilized and in Holland today (as in Italy) there are 100,000 elderly people in each million of the total population, with an anticipated rise to, say, 120,000 by AD 2000; in Great Britain, France, Belgium and West Germany, however, the present figure is about 130,000.

In the 1930s, when the idea of our modern form of welfare society began to emerge, people were looking backwards at some of the worst abuses of industrialization. The idea then was that after a lifetime of factory labour, so different from the earlier agrarian times when old men and women had their place in a more family-based style of life, people worn out by long years of drudgery deserved a period of rest and comfort. Moreover the illnesses of old age seemed then to be inescapable. Tuberculosis would kill and rheumatism would cripple – both complaints being to a large degree exacerbated by poor hygiene and bad housing. Things are different today.

In 1975 a large group of elderly people living in their own homes was studied in Scotland. It was found that the percentage needing some help in living a normal life was about a quarter of those aged between seventy and seventy-four, and about a third of those between eighty and eighty-four. At the age of eighty-five and over, most of them required support of one sort or another. Yet even so, three-quarters of the over-eighty-fives – after twenty and twenty-five years of life beyond the accepted age of 'retirement' – retained their ability to cope with the ordinary affairs of daily life provided they had appropriate help.

Incontinence

There are young people in their teens and early twenties who look forward with fear and dismay to the time when, they feel, they will be old, decrepit and useless. 'What shall we do,' they ask, 'when we are really old, say, thirty? Won't it be awful!' The more sensible among the young, quite apart from those of more mature age with the insight to understand that every age possesses its own peculiar rewards as well as its special disadvantages, can regard those naïve young people and their fears with a tolerant smile. It is equally true, however, that there are those of more advanced years who themselves look forward with even more fearful alarm to a future when, as they see it, they will be *really* old and (how could they face the disgrace?) incontinent.

In reply to such fears, there are two things to be said. The first is that few people, even among those in their eighties, ever suffer from incontinence and, secondly, among those who *do* become ill and incontinent, many are successfully treated and cured and many more will be in the future. It is important to note that of all those in the kingdom in 1965 who were aged sixty-five and over, 94 per cent lived normal lives in their own homes and only 1 per cent were hospitalized in psychiatric institutions. Only among this 1 per cent are the great majority of those suffering from incontinence to be found. It is important to understand that by far the commonest factor associated with incontinence is senile dementia. I shall discuss this in the next section of this chapter. While dementia is a serious condition, as will be recounted, it, too, is a minority affliction. Furthermore, while it still continues to rank as a grave form of illness among the aged, there are good reasons to anticipate that the rapid advances in scientific understanding now taking place may before long make it as rare in advanced communities as tuberculosis – the 'consumption' of the old days and, indeed, of days not all that long past. My own father died of tuberculosis in 1926.

The process of passing water is basically a reflex action. When the bladder of an infant or a young child is full, the reflex comes into play and he urinates. It is only later on, after a period of education, that he learns to exercise control over the process of urination. Should the brain be affected and dementia intervene, control over the bladder is lost. Those who retain their intellectual faculties, that is to say, the great majority of the elderly, have nothing to fear from this form of incontinence. There is even less cause for apprehension about another form of incontinence affecting older men. This can be due to an enlargement of the prostate gland which, in certain circumstances, may block the normal outflow of urine from the bladder and thus disturb the reflex action controlling micturition (the process of passing water). Should this occur, there are several effective medical and surgical remedies at hand. Women may suffer from a parallel and equally remediable condition. This may arise from a displacement – so called prolapse – of the uterus. Again, there are several effective methods of treatment available. There are other varieties of incontinence, some of which are, for example, due to the failure of the kidneys to function properly in their business of concentrating urine. Again, as is well known, steady progress has been made, and is still being made, in the prevention and treatment of kidney failure.

There is another apprehension which, while it cuts deep into the consciousness of those about to enter the ranks of the elderly, is far less justifiable than the fear of being run over while crossing the road: this is the fear of faecal incontinence. In fact, this condition is even more uncommon than urinary incontinence. Again, when it does occur, it is most frequently associated with mental confusion. People suffering from this may be unaware when their rectums are loaded. Faecal incontinence can also arise from such straightforward causes as over-eating; or in patients unthinkingly taking excessive doses of such medicaments as aperients, iron, antibiotics and the like, or even by treating themselves immoderately with sedatives so that they are not fully aware of what they are doing. A less common cause can be bowel infection. This is associated with diarrhoea. Nowadays, this can be tackled by isolating and identifying the infective micro-organism concerned and then treating the condition with the appropriate antibiotic. There are other rarer causes of faecal incontinence associated with particular complaints. For example, certain forms of damage to the spinal cord can interfere with the normal mechanism by which the bowel is controlled. Serious illness, particularly when a patient is delirious, may involve faecal incontinence, as can certain forms of diabetes. In general, however, the condition is comparatively rare and need not preoccupy the sensible elderly person who is concerned with the day-to-day doings of ordinary life, rather than with the less common features of ill health.

Senile dementia

While being comparatively rare, senile dementia is sufficiently serious and distressing to justify our giving every encouragement to those who are researching into its origins and mechanism so as to accelerate the very real promise which now exists that it can be brought under control. Any combination of elderly people aiming to exert themselves for the good of their less fortunate fellows could sensibly put high on their list of priorities the decision to encourage research into senile dementia. In doing so, not only would they benefit the unfortunate few who suffer from this disabling sickness during what it all too often causes to be the last few years of their lives, they would also do even more good to the families of the sufferers and to all those who attend to their wants – and who must so attend virtually every moment of the day and night. One of the saddest features of the complaint is the sorrow which those of any sensibility who serve the patients must experience. Part of the burden they bear is the knowledge that the actual patients themselves are often unaware of the pass to which they have come.

It is reasonable to estimate that about 1 per cent of elderly people come to require treatment in psychiatric hospitals and nursing homes and, of these, about 30 per cent may progress to the stage of dementia. It therefore appears that within the elderly group of the population (sixty-five and over) about 3 per 1,000 may eventually be affected. The disease, which mainly attacks people between seventy and eighty and is more common among women than men, involves a progressive loss of brain cells. It may start insidiously and then slowly progress or, on the other hand, some dramatic incident – an accident causing a broken leg, or a fever – may lead to a period of delirium followed by quite rapid intellectual deterioration. There is a similar condition, more common in elderly men, called arteriosclerotic dementia, which commonly arises in association with a stroke or a heart attack. The intellectual decline is in a series of steps rather than a continuous falling off as in senile dementia. The real problem with these dementias is that the sufferers are helpless and may be incontinent too. Like infants, they must be watched in every move, kept clean, dressed, undressed and fed. Most tragic of all, however, is the loss of personality and dignity and the knowledge that, when the condition is advanced, there are only about three years of life remaining – and life of total dependence and insensibility at that.

These conditions, namely senile dementia and arteriosclerotic dementia, although they only afflict a minority of the elderly, many of whom are very old, are serious illnesses which so far cannot be prevented. Anyone who has visited a hospital ward full of psychotic old people will have been saddened at their pitiful condition. They will also have recognized the fortitude and devotion of those whose duty it is to look after such patients. These sentiments are natural and commendable. There is, however, need for something more – more backing and encouragement for those involved in the scientific study and research into the dementias. Already, there is substantial evidence that success could be achieved, built on the progress that has already been made. But backing for the recruitment and support of researchers trained in the appropriate fields of learning is part only of what is needed. Equally important is the recognition by the public, as well as by medical and scientific specialists, of the importance of the quest and the rewards in both understanding and human happiness which would come from success.

The first important discovery that has been made, and which few people have so far grasped, is that senile dementia is a disease like any other and is gradually being understood; it is not simply part of the inevitable process of senescence and decay, like the withering of a dahlia cut off by the autumn frost. It is true that for the most part senile dementia afflicts those who are in their seventies or eighties, but it only strikes about 3 in every 1,000 of such. More remarkable than this, however, is the evidence to be derived from a condition called Alzheimer's disease. This is quite similar to senile dementia, yet it is a disease which attacks people in their forties and fifties. In fact, a case has been reported in a patient of fifteen, who died, as if in a state of what might carelessly be called advanced senility, at the age of twenty-four. The men and women contracting Alzheimer's disease – which is fortunately quite rare – may be at the height of their powers, in good health, and not in any way defective or senile. Nevertheless, symptoms of the disease insidiously appear. Slight defects in memory and behaviour become apparent. Perceptions of space and time become distorted. Mistakes begin to be made in dressing, eating, working and talking. Later on, as the disease advances, the sufferers become unable to speak intelligibly at all. What they say is a mere jumble of words. Quite often, they become restlessly active yet, in spite of their continual fretful busyness, they accomplish little. Alternatively, they may become lethargic. The disease progresses for five years, or perhaps for ten. Then, more often than not, the sufferers die in their fifties of what surely, viewing Alzheimer's disease for what it is – a pathological malfunctioning – we can no longer describe (as our predecessors once did) as 'old age'.

No community can will to make a scientific discovery just because they want to do so. Yet surely here is a condition which challenges the ingenuity and knowledge of scientific research. While the cause of Alzheimer's disease is as yet unknown, modern approaches to its elucidation offer promise that we are moving towards an understanding of the disease. At the very least, it is up to those who care, among whom surely is the new and potentially powerful group of the elderly, to make sure that adequate resources are deployed in appropriate research. Clinical research offers the new possibilities of psychiatry. For example, studies are in progress in this, as in senile dementia and other diseases, to determine whether the loss of memory which occurs is a failure to apprehend facts in the first place, a failure to retain such facts in the mind, or a failure to retrieve such facts as have been stored in the memory. Studies of this sort are of interest in themselves quite apart from the light which they can be expected to throw on special diseases. Consider the intellectual mechanism involved in memorizing a random number, for example, 149656941, and subsequently recalling it some time afterwards. This is a subtle process in which any failure can be attributed to a number of causes.

It is perhaps of some interest to pause for a moment to discuss the recollection of the above number as a general illustration of what goes on in any kind of memorizing. A moment's consideration shows that 149656941 is not a random number at all. A short scrutiny will show anyone with a historical bent that it is made up of the date 1496 written first forwards and then backwards with a 5 in the middle. The observation can be used to tie the set of numbers into the memory and helps those with an interest in the fifteenth century to recall it afterwards. Alternatively, for those with a mathematical interest, the figures can be seen to be a series of the last digits of the squares of the numerals 1, 2, 3, 4 and 5, followed by those of 4, 3, 2 and 1. No wonder children who have not had the opportunity to know either mathematics or history have difficulty in learning their tables!

There are many sorts of psychological studies which are being used to diagnose with increasing subtlety the changes in mental health which might be associated with the diseases which have now to be categorized as dementia. This line of attack can then be correlated with, for example, genetic and personality factors and with environmental and social stress.

To supplement clinical and psychological research in the attack on senile dementia there are today a number of powerful techniques, many of which have only recently been developed. One of the most dramatic of these is the EMI scanner. This elaborate instrument makes it possible to map out the cellular structure of the brain in great detail and in three dimensions. Studies are in progress to discover whether the degeneration accompanying dementia first attacks the brain cells themselves or occurs initially in the supporting tissues by which the structure of the brain is consolidated into a whole. There are several research groups hotly pursuing the clues from which, it is reasonable to hope, the cause and prevention of dementia may come.

There are diseases which are now known to possess a genetic component. One of these is gout; once a widespread scourge by no means restricted to those over-indulging in rich meats and port wine. Gout still occurs among those who are genetically susceptible to it. No longer, however, is it – as it once was – a major public health problem. While its onset cannot be stopped, scientific study has provided drugs by means of which its crippling symptoms and dreadful pain can be controlled. Tuberculosis was also known to strike more commonly those possessing a particular genetic make-up. It is only within our own lifetime that, due to discoveries in the scientific discipline of chemotherapy, this once dreaded horseman of the Apocalypse has been unseated. What, then, of a genetic factor in senile dementia? Clinical evidence has now demonstrated that the risk of dementia in advanced old age is four times as great for the relatives of those who have been afflicted than for those whose parents and grandparents have lived and died without being thus attacked.

Another point of advance through which progress may be made in the fight against the dementias has arisen from biochemical studies. It has been found that normal amounts of one of the chemical substances by which nerve impulses are transmitted are lacking in patients suffering from dementia. A parallel discovery which is being pursued with considerable enthusiasm in several laboratories is that there is a protein of a particular chemical configuration present in normally functioning brains which is found in lesser amounts or, perhaps, not at all in the brain cells of sufferers from dementia. Only in recent years, as the techniques for highly sophisticated chemical analysis has advanced hand in hand with those – of which the EMI scanner is an example – making possible even more sensitive physical study, has it been possible to advance subtle and incisive researches of this sort. Again it must be emphasized that the greatest good that the elderly could do, both for themselves, for the generations that follow them and for the community of which they are a significant component, would be to ensure that such researches are properly funded, adequately manned and pursued with zeal.

There are, too, studies of dementia in progress to discover whether a slow-acting virus or some toxic agent is involved. Little significant progress has been made in this direction, but a recent discovery has shown that when extracts of the brains of victims of certain rare forms of dementia affecting younger patients are injected into animals, the dementia is transmitted to the animals. This kind of research has also gone into the investigation of cancer which, like dementia, tends to be an ailment of later life. While no one has so far unequivocally identified a specific viral agent, it is now clear that many cancers are due to environmental agencies. Apart from the cumulative effect of cigarette smoking, it is now thought that contaminents in food may play a part in what happens long years later. The situation so far as dementia is concerned is less clear. Nevertheless, a tenuous hint has come to light which could perhaps incriminate aluminium. The hint arises from the experimental observation that aluminium can cause certain changes in those nerve cells classified as 'neuro-fibrillary tangles'. This observation, combined with tentative evidence that the trace amounts of aluminium naturally present in the brains of patients suffering from dementia are somewhat greater than those found in the brain tissues of unaffected old people, make it worth-while investigating the matter further.

Failing the identification of a virus involved in senile dementia, studies have been made to investigate the possibility that, in just the same way that some people – possibly for genetic reasons – are more susceptible than others to some particular disease organism, certain old people possess a less efficient immunological mechan-ism with which to protect themselves against whatever might be the cause of dementia.

Tissue culture is another specialized area of research which might possibly provide the key to the secret of dementia. It is the process whereby isolated pieces of living tissue are grown in an appropriate medium which, like the bloodstream of a healthy individual, provides the nutrients and the oxygen which the cells require for life, growth and multiplication. The life span of certain cells when grown thus in culture has been shown to be related to the age of the individual from whom they were taken. The question now to be answered is whether the longevity of individual cells is affected by the suscepti-bility of the donor to dementia. There are formidable technical difficulties in finding this out. Cellular ele-ments from the brain are difficult to maintain in culture, but it is not impossible to maintain them. Since the information to be won from them could be of such value, it is clearly important to encourage this line of research.

Thus we see that senile dementia is an affliction affecting only a small minority. Yet this is too many. Scientific promise, clearly apparent as research advances along a number of fronts, some of which I have just described, provides good hope of leading to the fuller understanding and eventual control of this disease – for such it is. Clearly it behoves a humane and educated community, spurred on if need be by the elderly, for they are at greatest risk, to stimulate a more urgent attack on this problem.

Cancer and diabetes

Although cancer and diabetes affect people of all ages, they are both more common in those of advanced years.

Cigarettes were once upon a time called 'coffin nails', but they do not cause cancer immediately. This is perhaps one of the main reasons why young people, in the pride of their youthful health and strength, are sometimes contemptuous of the warnings of their potential harmfulness; though with every year that passes the chances that a heavy smoker will contract cancer of the lung become stronger.

Cigarette smoking is, however, only one of the environmental hazards now known to be a potential cause of cancer in later life. Certain ingredients of food, naturally occurring or artificially incorporated, are now known to raise the odds of contracting cancer. Potential cancer-producing pollutants may be present in the atmosphere, and some of them, it now appears, may cause the disease many years later. Even oxygen itself, new evidence suggests, can encourage cancer in the end, while the young lovely who sunbathes in her bikini may, if she lives long enough, have cause to blame exposure to ultra-violet long ago for the cancer of her old age.

The challenge to science is threefold. First, to discover what might be carcinogenic and at what concentration. Second, to develop means whereby cancer, if it does occur, can be treated. Progress has been made in this field, although there is much more yet to know. The third challenge is one in which the doctors and their patients can usefully combine: we must breathe oxygen, go out in the sunshine, and eat food. How do we establish a balance between what is an acceptable risk and what we should control and avoid as unacceptable and reckless? Together with other members of the community, elderly people must take part in the debate.

Diabetes is a disease in which control over the system by which the sugar glucose, one of the main fuel supplies of the bodily engine, is regulated becomes disturbed. It is a comparatively common complaint. For example, there is a tribe of Red Indians among whom more than half of the over thirty-fives are diabetic. In Great Britain, taking the population as a whole, about 1 per cent, that is getting on for 650,000 people have diabetes, although probably half of these do not know that they have it. Progress in the treatment of the disease is of particular interest to the elderly because, although one can suffer from the malady at any age, 80 per cent of diabetics are over fifty and most of the new cases turn up in people between the ages of sixty and seventy.

The important point is that there are elderly people who feel unwell, who, perhaps, are often thirsty, or have trouble with their 'water-works', who are thin and wasted, who suffer the discomfort of soreness of the anus, discharging eyes and ulcers of the feet, who without knowing it, may be unduly susceptible to stroke and heart attack: such people may well be suffering from diabetes and once the disease is diagnosed, it can be brought under control, often by a mere adjustment of diet, and with its control all those debilitating symptoms listed above disappear. The lesson is clear. Modern understanding of diabetes is a further example of how scientific progress can convert an elderly suffering invalid back into an active useful citizen.

Stroke

At the age of seventy, about one person in nine of all those who die, dies of a stroke. Among those who survive until they are eighty, approximately one in six succumbs to the same cause. Nor does the proportion change much for those who survive beyond the age of eighty-five. Obviously, no matter how great the achievements of science, we all have to die of something; and while the prevention of stroke is a goal which it would indeed be eminently desirable to attain, the fact that strokes do occur could be taken as a lesser disgrace to human ignorance and the corresponding incapacity of medical science than that dementia is still capable of claiming its victims.

Stroke in its way, when it does not summarily kill, can be distressingly destructive of human personality. Nevertheless, victims of stroke can, in an increasing number of cases, be successfully treated and restored to some measure of – sometimes to virtually complete – effective activity. This, perhaps, is the most immediate promise of scientific research.

There are several kinds of stroke. Between the ages of forty-five and sixty cerebral haemorrhage – the bursting of one of the blood vessels in the brain – may take place. This is seen in decreasing numbers, possibly due to the treatment of high blood pressure in middle age. It is curious to note that cerebral haemorrhage is comparatively rare after the age of sixty. Most of the strokes to which elderly people – say those over sixty-five – are subject, are due to cerebral thrombosis. This is the partial or complete blockage of a blood vessel which cuts off the blood supply to one or other of the parts of the brain, thereby damaging the brain cells. Scientific and chemical understanding of how this comes about has already provided significant benefit to the current generation of the elderly. In most cases, a stroke in an elderly patient is associated with a *fall* in blood pressure. There may be all sorts of reasons for this; but there are now a number of procedures by which it is possible for the blood pressure to be controlled. Apart from the use of drugs, subtle and sophisticated though they are, perhaps the most productive application of scientific knowledge has been the use of the observation that the blood pressure of elderly people frequently falls – and thus increases the risk of their suffering a stroke – if they are kept in bed. The discovery that prolonged bed rest, at one time applied as a general panacea for almost any form of illness, can turn out to be dangerous for an elderly person has been productive of much good. Many strokes do, in fact, occur at night. The patient wakes up and, often with surprise, finds himself or herself stricken and partially paralysed. Although more massive strokes will render those who have suffered them deeply unconscious, there are patients less severely affected who may not at first realize that they have had a stroke at all. They may try to get up and in doing so fall and injure themselves further.

The realization that to send elderly patients to bed without cause, far from being to their benefit, can add to their problems, may not only lessen their susceptibility to stroke and other specific disabilities, but it may also contribute to a saner view of the capabilities of elderly people and of the responsibility which they share with everyone else of contributing to the creativity and vigour of the society of which they are members. This approach, if shared by the medical profession and by the elderly people, would of itself do much to promote health – there is more to it than the mere absence of disease and disability.

The promise that science holds for the elderly is probably best shown in the rising proportion of those who, having suffered a stroke and survived, are brought back into the main stream of the community to live useful and fully independent lives again. Current research has made significant advances towards treatment by which the blood pressure can be appropriately controlled. More highly developed systems of physical rehabilitation permit an increasing number of those who have suffered a stroke to use to the maximum the unaffected portion of their brain. Finally, it has been discovered that people who have recovered from a stroke, who were once upon a time thought to be incapable of anything but the most limited physical exertion, can not only stand up to much more vigorous physiotherapy than was once thought, but also are greatly benefited therefrom.

As I have explained, a stroke, by cutting off, either partially or completely, the flow of blood to some portion of the brain, damages the cells by depriving them of their life-support. Studies have been made of the subsequent performance of the parts of the brain so deprived. Sometimes the cells are permanently harmed, sometimes a significant degree of recovery is achieved, and sometimes a complete recovery is made. Apart from this research aimed at assessing the factors which determine whether brain damage is reversible or irreversible, a great deal is now known about the geography of the brain and the precise parts which control each of the diverse functions of the body. For example, it has long been known that when the left side of the brain is affected, it is the right side of the body that is paralysed, and vice versa. A more subtle point, however, is that the side of the brain which controls speech is determined by whether the individual is left-handed or right-handed. Perhaps even more curious is the corollary: ambidextrous people, who can use their left and their right hands equally well, possess the added advantage over their fellows that they are less likely to lose their powers of speech should they suffer a stroke. It appears that they possess, as it were, a spare speech area in their brains.

Present scientific knowledge cannot prevent stroke, but already it seems likely that the chances of being affected will be reduced. It is certainly true that scientific understanding can contribute to the rehabilitation of those who do suffer and at the same time reinforce the new lesson which all elderly people should learn, namely that they are tougher and more capable of physical endeavour than they have thought in the past. By thinking of themselves as frail, the elderly have encouraged the community at large to treat them as inferior citizens who may be allowed to subsist on half-pay.

Hypothermia

Hypothermia is a condition from which elderly people can suffer. It has been drawn to public attention by a variety of concerned groups during the last few years. While scientific promise can now clearly point to a number of ways by which hypothermia may be overcome, the most direct solution to perhaps more than half of the problem is sociological rather than strictly scientific. Hypothermia, like most malnutrition, though based on a deficiency – of heat for hypothermia and of one vitamin or another for malnutrition – is commonly due to poverty. Few rich old ladies suffer from hypothermia; it is the poor old ladies whose cases more often get into the newspapers. This is the first point which, now that it is understood, offers promise of better things ahead.

But while this is so, there are at the same time signs that hypothermia could be mastered by scientific means. The state of affairs at present is that each year in England and Wales about 400 elderly people die from hypothermia. Detailed studies of elderly patients coming into hospitals for a number of reasons showed that some of them were suffering from hypothermia without being aware of the fact. It was calculated that during the three months, February, March and April, during which the study was in progress, 9,000 cases of hypothermia were diagnosed. Further investigation showed that as people grow older there is a tendency for their temperature to fall. The current thinking is that it is quite possible that the temperature of about 1 in 10 of all elderly people living at home may be 35°C–35.5°C (that is 95°F or just above that level) or below. In fact, these people may have hypothermia without knowing it.

This complaint is quite different from what is commonly called 'primary' hypothermia – in a properly run society it ought not to be allowed to exist. Primary hypothermia occurs at any age when the ambient environment is so cold that the body's thermal mechanism is unable to maintain the physiologically optimum temperature of 37°C (once called 98.4°F). Climbers whose clothes have become wet and who are exposed to a strong chill wind may die of cold – that is of hypothermia. Shipwrecked sailors plunged into the ice-cold waters of the Arctic seas will succumb from the same cause. With elderly people whose sense of cold has become blunted and whose capacity to generate heat to maintain their body temperature has diminished, the most important discovery that has been made is that they need an ambient temperature of 21.1°C (which is 70°F). Any British reader over the age of, say, fifty years, brought up in the Spartan belief that 'room temperature' was 60°F (that is 15.5°C) and that open windows all the year round were healthy, will appreciate how significant is the scientific discovery about the underlying cause of what could be called pathological hypothermia, and how different this condition is from primary hypothermia.

The basic cause of such hypothermia, it is now recognized, can be a chilly environment, and not so very chilly at that. A study carried out in the 1970s showed in England and Wales in the winter the temperature of the living rooms of 10 per cent of elderly people was lower than 12°C (that is 54.4°F). There are in existence official regulations, for example, those of the Factory, Offices and Railway Premises Act, laying down by law the minimum temperature deemed acceptable for working people in a well regulated society. It can now be seen that a parallel set of regulations are needed as an essential public health measure to protect elderly people against hypothermia. This is one step based on scientific advance, which could be taken to remove a potential threat to older people.

There is, however, still need for further research. When a healthy person becomes cold and his body temperature falls, he starts to shiver. This muscular vibration produces heat by which, under normal and not too extreme circumstances, the situation is remedied. In those elderly people who are potential victims of hypothermia, the shivering response is impaired. When they are in a cold environment, their body temperatures steadily fall. Studies of healthy people of the same age showed that under the same circumstances although they *felt* cold, their body temperatures were in fact maintained at the normal level. Clearly, something other than the unfavourable conditions of their environment is amiss with those who are susceptible to hypothermia. There is need for further research into the nature of the breakdown of the shivering mechanism, but already there are signs that progress is being made. For example, there are certain drugs, among which the phenothiazines are one group, which cause the blood vessels to dilate. One effect of this is to abolish shivering. It is the loss of shivering, as a signal that they are becoming cold, as well as a contributor to the correction of the coldness, that permits the temperature of hypothermia patients to fall without their knowledge. Alcohol is a drug which possesses a somewhat similar effect. People who take a 'stiff drink' to warm themselves up may find their hands and feet warmer due to the dilation of peripheral blood vessels. In fact, however, the loss of heat from their bodies as a whole is increased, and if at that moment they are exposed to conditions which could cause primary hypothermia the alcohol will lessen their resistance. It is possible, therefore, that studies of the mechanism by which drugs such as the phenothiazines affect the control of body temperature will provide a clue to the reasons for physiological susceptibility to hypothermia.

There are other potentially fruitful avenues for scientific attack, too. For example, reduced activity of the pituitary gland, so called hypopituitarism, is known to upset the thermoregulatory mechanism. It is also well recognized that the condition known as myxoedema, in which the activity of the thyroid is disturbed and the whole life process of the body slowed down, is associated with an abnormally low body temperature.

What would appear to be a promising approach is the research concerned with the relationship between body temperature and its regulation and brain function. There are neurological disorders in which thermoregulation is known to be affected. Following certain strokes, for example, it has been found that control of the body temperature may be disturbed.

As in so many forms of illness, the prevention and cure of hypothermia can clearly be seen to be an inextricable amalgam of scientific understanding of the physiological mechanisms involved, the discovery of the means to put right what is discovered to be wrong and, just as important, the weaving of such scientific knowledge into a social fabric in which economic and environmental factors are of parallel importance. Cold living conditions and the lack of sufficient money or love and attention are an inherent part of one set of factors from which hypothermia may arise. Another set of factors, however, comprises the still-not-fully-understood question of why it is that of two people of the same age and condition one is not able to react appropriately to cold and the other is. Nor is hypothermia always a problem on its own. It may, as an added complication, be linked with dementia, with crippling conditions by which patients are immobilized or, as I have just mentioned, with stroke. Nevertheless, here again it is surely not an exercise in irrational optimism to conclude that science, combined with the necessary drive to get things done, offers hope of progress.

Diseases of the joints

Ten per cent of all the men and 1 per cent of all the women over the age of sixty-five suffer from one or other of the disabilities of the joints. They therefore have good reason to use such influence as they command in the support of all scientific research which might lead to an improvement in the situation.

Scientific *promise* there may be. It must, however, be said that effective *performance* – that is the knowledge and facilities to prevent the considerable amount of disability and distress that must today be attributed to malfunction of the joints in elderly people – is not within easy reach. Nevertheless, what has been achieved is worth reviewing.

Osteoarthritis is the gradual stiffening of the joints which overtakes some elderly people until their spines, their hips, knees, elbows and the joints of their fingers gradually seize up. Is this due to a disturbance of the blood flow, or to 'general metabolic disorder' (whatever that may be)? Is it caused by one or more of the body's hormones, or by genes? All these possibilities have been suggested. Meanwhile, the sufferers must do the best they can with aspirin, a good diet to prevent their becoming too heavy, physiotherapy and encouragement. Finally, there is the possibility of help from so-called bioengineering. Mechanical joints of all sorts, for the hip, the knee, the fingers, of ever increasing versatility and refinement, are being designed and installed, and the likelihood of their prolonged and satisfactory perfor-mance is gradually increasing. Yet while we admire the surgeons and engineers for their skill, and for the great relief they can bring, the target must still be to understand and prevent the diseases which make them necessary. Osteoarthritis is one such disease, rheumatoid arthritis is another. If American statistics can be taken to have general applicability, about 2 in every 100 old people may end up crippled by the rheumatoid arthritis from which they suffered in middle life and which nobody was able to cure. Gout is also a form of arthritis, in that it affects the joints, and not only the joints of the big toe. Furthermore, like rheumatoid arthritis, it is another joint disease which elderly people share with those who are not elderly at all. I have a friend in the prime of life, and a very talented man he is too, who has had gout for years. It cannot be cured but modern treatment is so effective that the malady is not allowed to interfere with his creative activities. Gout, however, may be a cause of special concern to the elderly because in later life it can settle down into a chronic disability.

It is in many respects an interesting disease. It is also an example of a condition which has been studied for many years. The fact that one hears so little about it today compared with the widespread attention attracted by it in earlier times is not because it has been stamped out but because present scientific knowledge enables it to be kept firmly under control.

The facts about gout are these. Its immediate cause is the formation of abrasive crystals of the naturally occurring body component uric acid in the affected. joint. Gout possesses a strong genetic component, that is, it runs in families. Hormones also have something to do with it as is shown by the fact that it is twenty times as common in men as it is in women and, as was first pointed out by Hippocrates, that it never occurs in eunuchs. It has long been thought that there is a link between eating and drinking, particularly eating and drinking to excess without taking adequate physical exercise, and attacks of gout – but only in people who are susceptible to the disease. Then again, the amount of uric acid and its compounds found circulating in the blood stream of gout patients is slightly greater than it is in the blood of non-susceptible people of the same age. There is, however, a good deal of overlap between the two groups. Suspicion has also been directed towards the possibility that the kidneys of gout sufferers might be less efficient either in letting surplus uric acid escape from the body or in preventing what is being passed through the kidneys from being pumped back into the circulation again. Nothing much, however, has come of these suggestions.

What *can* be done to deal with this form of arthritis is to build on the knowledge of the past in treating it when it does occur. While this does not provide the solution to the problem of how to prevent gout – or any other arthritis, either in elderly people or in those who are not elderly at all – it does make it possible to combat its effects. For more than two hundred years, colchicine, a drug derived from the autumn crocus, has been recognized as a potent remedy. Benjamin Franklin introduced the flower into America to provide a supply of colchicine there for the treatment of gouty settlers. Colchicine apparently prevents the formation of the irregularly shaped crystals of uric acid which hamper the movement of the affected joints and cause the intense pain so characteristic of the disease. A more modern drug, probenicid, introduced in 1962, attacks the malady from another direction. Its effectiveness comes from the fact that it restricts the activity of the kidneys in returning some of the uric acid that passes through them back into the system. This leads to a gradual diminution of the working pool of uric acid in the body.

Whether it comes later or earlier in life, arthritis of one sort or another must be borne with. Science, though it cannot prevent, can do something to alleviate the situation.

Respiratory diseases

Although active elderly people cannot look to science for a promise that such respiratory diseases as bronchitis and pneumonia will be done away with tomorrow, at least they can have the satisfaction of knowing that – as with arthritis – *something* can be done to alleviate these conditions. They themselves, however, must be prepared to combat the diseases in the ways which are open to them.

An elderly man can avoid the distresses of 'old man's cough' (which, all too often, contributes to the 12 per cent of deaths from respiratory disease among elderly hospital patients) by giving up smoking, or smoking much less, before he becomes elderly.

Science has provided us with one particularly potent weapon for the fight against bronchitis in the elderly – it is central heating. The installation of central heating in the bedrooms of susceptible elderly patients would safeguard them during the damp and foggy nights of winter. It is sensible and proper in a cool and rainy climate such as that of Great Britain that the houses of the elderly be equipped in this way. After all, we do not expect children to go about without the shoes they need to keep their feet warm, why, therefore, should their grandparents be expected to sleep in bedrooms which are not adequately heated?

As with so many problems, hope for the future must come partly from the advances being made in medical science and partly from the decisions made by concerned people about the kind of lives they want and the measures they are prepared to take. The installation of central heating in the houses of the elderly would demand the deployment of the necessary economic resources. Be it so. The minor complaint of chilblains, widespread in my youth, has been virtually done away with by a corresponding improvement in the standard of living of the community. If this was achieved by organizing warmer winter conditions in the last generation, let the further steps be taken to reduce the incidence of the much more serious condition of bronchitis.

We must sadly admit that at present science can do little to cope with the recurrent chest colds which are a further factor in the incidence of bronchitis. It seems, therefore, that like everybody else, the elderly will have to put up with coughs and colds and wait until scientific understanding finds a way of coping – as it is reasonable to hope it will – with viruses and with the miscellaneous organisms which continue to bedevil bronchitis of any age.

Strictly speaking, pneumonia, the other main disease of the lungs, is the condition of waterlogging and collapse in a lung following infection by various bacteria. It can affect young people as well as old ones. There is, however, a variant of pneumonia, sometimes associated with bronchitis, which can bring down elderly people who are weak, static and being kept in bed. The ways of tackling this complaint in the future may differ from the present form of treatment. There is already knowledge available to combat the pneumococci which are involved, to drain off the affected parts of the lungs, to adjust the fluid balance of the tissues, and to do much else to maintain the weak, elderly bed-ridden patient. It now seems, however, that this may not always be the wisest approach. There may be many occasions when the people concerned decide that they are no longer willing to submit with resignation to being patients. Those who decline to stay in bed – possibly because they are too busy – do not become bed-ridden. And perhaps if they are up and about and, not being half asleep, give a few good coughs, the infected secretion which would otherwise accumulate in their lungs and give them pneumonia will not do so!

Heart attacks

None of us has complete control over what is going to happen. Nevertheless, it is open to anyone – and not least to an elderly person – to assert with the poet, 'I am the master of my fate, I am the captain of my soul'.* Such a one is well aware that everyone must die of something and, if well informed, may also know that about half of all those who die over the age of seventy-five die of heart disease. If they are better informed still, however, they may also know that, if the scientific understanding we now have were sensibly applied to the problem of heart attacks among the elderly, there is a good chance that the expectation of life would be extended by ten years. Perhaps what is particularly striking and important – possibly even more so than in combating bronchitis and pneumonia – is that if elderly people would only take the trouble to comprehend the scientific discoveries about heart disease and do something about it themselves, they could forthwith improve their own situation and prolong their lives.

For example, what the laity call 'coronaries', which are more accurately described as ischaemic heart disease (ischaemic implying a failure in the blood supply to the heart), can, to a significant degree, be prevented if potential patients lead the right kind of life, both when they are already elderly and beforehand. To avoid – or certainly to postpone – a heart attack, all the elderly person must do is (a) be busy and physically active, (b) not eat too much and thus become fat, (c) avoid too much butter and cream, fried food, fat meat and rich cakes, and (d) avoid smoking too much. These rules apply to women as well as to men; although eight times as many middle-aged men suffer heart attacks as

* The poet, by the way, was William Henley (1849–1903).

middle-aged women, and even in later life when the risks are much greater for both men and women, an elderly man is still eight times as likely to suffer a heart attack as an elderly woman.

While scientific understanding now shows the extent to which elderly people can help to avoid heart attacks by leading full lives (or, in other words, by avoiding what was once categorized as the deadly sin of laziness), science itself can do much too. The promise so far is not that heart disease will *never* occur, but that much can be done to recognize what is happening and to minimize its effects. As a simple example, there is the current recognition that the condition of angina pectoris, which warns a younger patient by its sharp pain not to overtax his heart, may not send such a warning to an older patient, who merely feels breathless and fatigued. By recognizing this, the older patient, too, can avoid putting undue strain on his heart. Or when ischaemia, by cutting down the blood supply to the heart, upsets the electrical mechanism by which in health its even beat is maintained, the bio-engineer can provide a mechanical pacemaker by which the breakdown can be remedied.

Perhaps the most important thing the doctor, making use of scientific knowledge, can do for an elderly person whose heart is failing to function according to his or her needs – this is so-called 'congestive heart failure' – is to recognize what the problem is, and to realize that the shortness of breath, swelling of the ankles, coughing and tiredness are not, as is sometimes assumed, mere indications of senility, but the symptoms of heart failure which can be put right.

Disease of the kidneys

In my discussion of the promise of science to provide a good life in the extra years it is now giving this generation I can touch appropriately on the degree to which it can today ensure properly functioning kidneys. The truth of the matter is that as life goes on the kidneys, like so many other organs of the body – the eyes, the ears, the lungs, the heart – although adequate, it is to be hoped, for the duties imposed on them, become less effective than they were. This is hardly surprising since the kidneys are quite subtle and remarkable organs. They carry out two interesting and complex functions. On the one hand, they filter a variety of compounds out of the blood and allow them to pass from the body in the urine. The principal compound they deal with in this way is urea, which is derived from the protein we are nowadays so proud of eating but which, in the main, we simply burn up for fuel. If for any reason our kidneys fail to perform this function properly, we are in serious trouble which may call for the application of science in its most elaborate form, as dialysis equipment or kidney transplantation. This, however, is not primarily a problem for the elderly. They are more likely to be concerned with the second function of the kidneys. This is that after having allowed the more liquid fraction of the blood to pass through the filter they provide, the kidneys must then, once the potentially toxic ingredients have escaped, pump back into the system the appropriate proportions of substances which the body does need. If the kidneys cannot perform this function efficiently, the urine will be more dilute than it should be. An undue amount of water will then escape from the body and the patient will become dehydrated unless, that is, he or she knows what is happening and does something about it.

Now we have come full circle. At the beginning of this chapter, it was pointed out how unjustified was the nagging fear of incontinence with which all too many people in the past have made themselves apprehensive and miserable without cause. There are far more important and creative things to do, in the current climate of scientific knowledge, than worry thus. On the other hand, for well organized elderly people, determined to make a contribution to their generation within the new freedom provided by science, understanding of the basis of the problems of dehydration allows them to provide what, in the majority of cases will prove to be their own solution. This is to have the courage to drink more water. Water lost from the body because of inefficient functioning of the kidneys cannot be restored if elderly people, either from lack of confidence or – it must be said – from laziness (a reluctance to get up in the night to pass water), will not drink the water they need.

How better can this chapter finish than in a call for courage, vigour and the use of scientific knowledge to encourage the elderly not to become dehydrated?

3 Where We Are Now

There is a lot to be said for being old. Children look forward to being grown up. Students, in spite of the attention which is attracted by their fringe activities, often work hard to obtain the qualifications which they feel they need to ensure them a rewarding place in the community later on. Apprentices put up with low wages and subordinate status in order to acquire skills to serve them in good stead afterwards. Young couples will burden themselves with mortgages. The Parliamentary Secretary endures drudgery in the expectation of future rewards. Surely, therefore, elderliness is the best period in life: when people have it all, when the fruit on these trees has ripened and the harvest has been gathered in, when the lucky old own their own houses or pay derisory rents fixed years before, when some of them are directors of companies, others Ministers of the Crown, matrons of hospitals, headmistresses, responsible and skilled workers in factories, trades union leaders and chairpersons of women's institutes. Surely the elderly are to be envied as having arrived at happiness.

The fact that many elderly people do not see themselves as belonging to an outstandingly fortunate category of citizenry is partly because they have not realized their own potentialities – both physical and political – in the present age of science and, equally, because the community as a whole has not fully woken up to the situation either. In 1978, the Department of Health and Social Security brought out an admirably intentioned 'discussion document' entitled 'A Happy Old Age'. Its aims were, firstly, to try to organize affairs so that the elderly could live in comfort and health without having to make any exertion themselves. The second stated intention was to keep them active but out of the way at home. The generally accepted implication of this target is, of course, that the elderly should be taken out of the main stream of social life where the real action is. Kindly meant though this may be, it misses the main points which are that by sending them home regardless of the twenty years extra that science now gives them, the poverty of the elderly is – if not ensured – made more probable and their happiness compromised. The third intention of the Government's discussion document was to involve the elderly in decisions made about their status and social function. This, indeed, is a challenge which should be taken up in the light of what is being accomplished in this remarkable historical period in which the scientific chickens are coming home to roost and changing both the texture of society and the medical and physiological status of the elderly who must establish their role in it.

Regardless of what people say and the attacks they make on the troubles and worries of the daily round, their life's happiness is primarily built, so far as the majority of ordinary citizens are concerned, around their work. Childhood, school, training and experience are all directed to the purpose of getting a job. The question we first ask a stranger on becoming acquainted with him is 'What do you do for a living?' It was once legitimate to answer – but no more – 'I am a man of independent means'. 'What are you?' must be answered by 'I am a fitter . . . a stock broker . . . a brain surgeon'. And even if the answer is, 'I am a single-handed Atlantic-crossing sailor', or a 'bird watcher', it is always assumed that there is money to be earned from a newspaper or a university for doing such things.

Employment – that is, the earning of money through some activity – brings happiness in three ways. The first is from the money it provides. The second is the joy of possessing an ability, that is, the skill, knowledge and dexterity to do whatever the job involves. And the third is the social satisfaction of an organized life in combination with other people; enjoying the exchange of a cheery greeting with the postman, the co-operation of workmates, the talk at the tea break, the discussions with the foreman, the salesmen's conference, the shared experiment in the laboratory, and the drink after hours in the pub. In the modern world of high technology, with its inter-locking complexities powerfully impelling every organization, book publishers, local authorities, motor-car factories, doctors in group practices, to mention only a few, to move towards a bigness in which the individual is the only unit that remains the same size, most people need, for their happiness, to be part of some bigger organization. That is to say, they need a job.

There are two non-answers to the question, 'What do you do for a living' (or even 'What are you?'). They are, 'I am unemployed', or, to express the same thing in the form of words conventionally considered applicable to a particular time of life, 'I am retired'. This answer and the feelings it evokes in the society of today, have a deep significance. So far as his condition of life is concerned, a man could have replied with equal truth, as his Victorian or Edwardian predecessor would have done, 'I am a man of independent means'. His means of living, such as they are, are indeed independent of any weekly pay packet or monthly salary cheque for which he has to labour. Regardless, however, of the adequacy or inadequacy of the means, he – or she – does not think of it in that way. The loss of status, of money, of seniority, prestige and authority is hard. Having been part of the great factories, the powerful companies, the hotel chains, corporate life-blood of the community – its government, its power, railways, coal mines and of the posts by which — more than ever in this age of electronics — the social body is held together and made to work, how can we blame a thoughtful man of sixty-five, or a woman of sixty, from feeling other than deflated at being excluded from the real working of the state? There *is* another point of view, but let us remain for the time being with this one.

In reflecting on this postulated twenty years of active life from about sixty to eighty, the elderly know that for many people now these years are unsatisfactory. They are, to my mind, unsatisfactory not so much because of physical and material deficiency — because some of the elderly are ill, cold, rheumatic and breathless, and some of them are poor — but much more because of the way in which they are excluded from the main stream of daily life, because of the way the rest of the community thinks about them and, perhaps most damaging of all, because of the way they think about themselves.

The sixty-five-year-old man, yesterday an active worker with, as we have already discussed, an organized, systematic, familiar routine, today finds himself with a less compulsive, different schedule of activities. He gets up later than he was accustomed to do; he takes the dog for a walk, if the current emphasis on environmental purity has left him with a dog; he strolls round the corner to talk to a crony in a situation similar to his own; he comes in to dinner which, in the economic straits of retirement, is not a very exciting meal. For the afternoon, there is a little gardening, the dog to take for another walk, perhaps there is a visit to the public library or to the old folks' club. There are other occupations, of course. There is painting the back door, attending to the garden (if there is a garden). Then there are games and hobbies: pursuits which a year before, when life was real, gave amusement to an idle hour. Activities which during the economically productive period of life were fitted into non-working times are now expanded into the major events – the high spots – of the day. Friday's visit to the post office to collect the pension money; making a journey to town (using the free bus permit issued to old folks) to buy a new shirt; an afternoon's bingo – these are what now must serve to occupy the mind of a man who, so short a time ago, was head of a department, or the driver of an underground train responsible for the lives of three hundred people.

This is perhaps too simple a picture. The organization of a bus outing can involve endless meetings, prolonged discussion and complex and laborious administrative detail. Bell-ringing, bowls and brass bands at one end of the social scale are balanced by golf, bridge and the organization of an environmental protection society at the other.

Up till now, such a largely empty and trivial life style for retired people has been tacitly accepted both by the still active younger community and by the elderly themselves. That this should be so has been justified by a number of intellectual schools within the scientific discipline of sociology. On the one hand is the 'functionalist' school, which works on the assumption that the main function of a man's life is to maximize the industrial productivity of the community. A man who lives his whole life in the village where his family and all his relations have lived for generations, and where he may hope to enjoy a useful old age, is not meeting the need of factories for mobility of labour. If he will not leave his home to work at the new motor-car factory fifty miles away he loses his function in a society where motor-car factories are paramount. The sociological theory of 'functionalism' further insists that the social usefulness of the young man or woman is determined by the skills and qualifications which fit him or her to become a unit of the work force suited to the changing needs of the industrial community. Obviously, the older worker, with a head full of obsolete training, showing resistance to the ever accelerating introduction of technological novelty, and exhibiting continuously failing ability to acquire the new skills needed for the new techniques, can only be recognized as possessing a function which is continuously diminishing in importance. Little wonder that the cool intellectual approach of this sociological theory impels those who adopt it to conclude that these older workers – their social function having wasted away – should be removed from the system altogether.

Another school of sociological thought also supports our current consensus in favour of retirement for the elderly. This school comprises protagonists of the hypothesis of 'disengagement'. The aging individual, or so it is postulated, disengages himself from his work, from his colleagues at work and, as time goes by, from the whole active life of his community. 'Disengagement' – so runs this sociological hypothesis in its somewhat obscure prose – 'is a triple withdrawal: a loss of roles, a contraction of contacts and a decline in the commitment to norms and values.'

Neither of these hypotheses has been universally accepted either by sociologists or by others who, not claiming to be scientists, have thought about the matter. Perhaps the theory of 'withdrawal' has been most vigorously attacked. The scientific evidence supporting it is not very strong and, moreover, it would perhaps be altogether too convenient for those who, for their own reasons, would be only too glad to argue that they were doing the old person a good turn: industrialists only too pleased, perhaps, to find an excuse to get rid of an argumentative fellow director or an autocratic manager, or to replace an expensive senior worker by a cheaper younger one, or trades union organizers trying to justify getting rid of older workers in order to free the jobs they have filled for so long by other union members who are out of work. Why should any one bother to find alternative occupation for the elderly if the' theory of 'withdrawal' implies that a contraction of interests and a disengagement from the ordinary affairs of life is a natural process which is an inherent part of aging? The scientific protagonists can go further. Why bother to do anything about the loneliness and isolation of the inevitably unemployed old people if they are merely symptoms of withdrawal? This kind of rationalization can be taken further and used to justify the low economic status of the elderly which is imposed partly on the assumption – which the disengagement hypothesis would certainly seem to support – that there is no harm in condemning old people to frugality because they do not need as much as the young; the real truth of the matter is that the finances of the community need to be organized so as to provide the necessary funds to protect the old from penury.

So far, in looking at the state of the elderly in today's society, I have pointed out that, while they are in many respects fortunate, for example, in often owning their own houses and possessing, in the form of their pension, a private income, some to them may, on the other hand, feel deprived because of being shunted into a siding out of the busy trunk-road of life. Nevertheless, common kindness, reinforced, it is true, by some measure of self-interest and supported by sociological theories boasting at least a modest proportion of evidential credibility, must be given credit for having led to a major social effort to give the elderly a comfortable period of leisure to reward them for their years of work. But is this what they want? Many of them do. The alternative to the desire to continue to contribute to the purpose, drive and achievement of the society of which they are members is, indeed, the wish to withdraw and be happily and comfortably idle.

Many people, during most of their later life, would, if the opportunity were presented to them, be in a position to choose which they would prefer to engage themselves in – work or leisure. But there may be a time when illness and advanced old age make creative activity, whether it is designated work or otherwise, no longer possible. It is only natural, in the humane social climate of Great Britain that a great deal of attention be given to the provision of health services to cater for the special needs of this group of elderly people. Such services must be accepted for this minority of the elderly, even though the amount of attention devoted to them may sometimes suggest to those of the elderly who are not ill that they should perhaps be preparing for that eventuality.

The practicalities for the community of making the elderly comfortable have involved a number of issues. Many local authorities provide free travel on buses. The nationalized railways have a special scheme for fare concessions. Campaigns have been initiated to ensure that the step on to a bus shall be less than fifteen inches high and that places shall be kept free so that when elderly people do get on to the buses there is always somewhere for them to sit down. There are concerned groups who worry about how to provide public transport in country areas where most people go by car and buses are few; there are others who agitate for the installation of sheltered seats where the elderly can wait out of the rain for such buses as there are, and that some way can be worked out to help them with their parcels and luggage.

Not all elderly people can expect to be always in good health, any more than can all those who are not elderly. Over and above the ordinary share of illness which the elderly may be expected to suffer, however, they must expect to encounter disabilities peculiar to their age which as they get older and older, will outweigh the hardships – such as German measles and road accidents – which more particularly afflict the young. It follows, therefore, that the practical politics of today are involved with increasing the numbers of health visitors, nurses and physiotherapists employed and paid by the community to visit elderly people in their homes – or at least to be readily available to them. There are also more detailed matters about which political pressures are often brought to bear. For example, there is the provision of vehicles and drivers to transport elderly people who are unable to move about without difficulty from their houses to the various clinics and services which the community makes available to them. Public attention is also paid to the best way to train the receptionists at doctors' surgeries and health centres so that they can efficiently and kindly work out whose need is most urgent and give tolerant attention to those who come to the centres for company and conversation.

There is, too, the provision of chiropodists, of hot meals-on-wheels, as they are called, delivered to the door, of home helps and of an advisory service to arm the elderly against too credulously believing advertisements persuading them to spend their money on inessential articles that they cannot properly afford. Finally, although some of the elderly are fortunate in the unembarrassed possession of the family home which they have pertinaciously struggled to acquire during their working life, there are others who, when they are compelled by the community to retire from the ranks of the main-stream 'work force', find themselves in need of somewhere to live. Considerable political attention is given to assessing the numbers of the elderly lacking a proper place to live, in considering what kind of place would best suit their needs, how many rooms they require, how best they can be heated, what cooking facilities should be installed, where such housing ought to be, whether it should be in the hurly-burly of the city's centre where the elderly inmates can look out on the busy world or whether they would be better off in some leafy retreat in privacy and quiet, perhaps above the clamour of the day at the top of a tower enjoying all the comforts and conveniences of modern housing technology. 'Research', according to Age Concern, 'should be undertaken into developing a series of objective criteria for standards of domicillary care.'

Schemes and ideas are diverse. There are various plans whereby elderly couples shall be able to obtain housing appropriate to their needs and physical capacity. Further plans have been worked out whereby the community provides sums of money to be given to elderly people whose houses are old, inappropriate and in poor repair to enable them to get them renovated and improved. There are schemes to allow elderly people to exchange the house they live in for another which is either more convenient for them or in better repair or, alternatively, which is situated in a more favoured place or, perhaps, is nearer to a son or daughter or an old friend.

Perhaps the topic to which more attention has been given than any other is that of economics. The elderly are a significant group within the population: their number has increased markedly in the last thirty years and science already enables them to enjoy a substantial degree of health and vigour. Society, however, has decided that the elderly should be withdrawn from the category of those citizens who contribute to the wealth of the community, and, having ceased to do so, they cannot be rewarded, as are their fellow members, by being paid accordingly. The question consequently arises: do the elderly enjoy a sufficient income to enable them to live in comfort and enjoy this rosy period of contentment for which the whole of their earlier life has been a preparation? What the community is asking, and what political parties, one after the other, in their bid for favour are seeking to ensure – or so at least, they try and persuade themselves, and those whose support they desire – is that the income that society has organized for its elderly members does (as far as it can be achieved on earth) make the age of retirement a worthy interlude between the mundane battle of working life and the heaven which will succeed it.

The question was answered in an admirable study published in 1977,* which analysed the available official information on the British population and took into account family expenditure surveys carried out between 1968 and 1973, and an annually recurring investigation of 30,000 people. It was, perhaps, a surprising answer to some of those who, immersed in their vigorous endeavours for the good of old people and well knowing that support is most readily obtained when the flesh of those whose co-operation is desired can be made to creep, had overlooked the magnitude of the progress that had been made towards the desired state of affairs. This state – the purpose of the policy – is the provision of happy idleness for the elderly.

It may seem difficult in equity to justify on the one hand acceding to the argument of a working man of sixty-four – or the much more persuasive argument of a combination of some thousands of such men – that a tolerable life can only be supported on a basic weekly wage of £75, or whatever the topical figure may be at the time of the argument, and at the same moment to fix the pension of the same man on his sixty-fifth birthday at £28 a week. Yet when the survey data were studied in detail, the following figures emerged. When the household incomes of all the working members of the community were assessed and then combined with the household incomes of those who were unemployed but not elderly, it emerged that the average household of 3.2 people lived on an income of £84.30 a week. This represents £26.31 a head. For retired people, the income varied from a low point of £21.35 per head for a

* *Profiles of the Elderly*, Age Concern Res. Pub., 1977.

two-person family to a high of £25.48 per week for a man over sixty-five living by himself. These sums are less than what the average non-retired person has to live on, but they are not drastically less. The same comparatively small differences were also found when the average weekly expenditures – on housing, fuel, light, food, clothing and all the other items which come into a family budget – were compared. The average weekly expenditure per person for households of non-retired people came out at £19.58 and for retired people at £18.14. This was in 1975. Undoubtedly, when the age of retirement comes, the people passing across the watershed need to steel themselves for a shock. If the average incomes of people at different stages in life are calculated separately, it will be found that if the amount of money available to the eighteen to forty-five age group is taken as 100, the income available to the forty-five to fifty-nine age group will be 136. It is this figure that comes down with a bump to 80 for retired people who are sixty years old and older.

The situation is more complicated than it looks, though average values are, of course, useful; for there are people poorer (as well as richer) than the average. Particular circumstances also affect the issue. I have already mentioned that many elderly people have, through their efforts when young, come to own a house. The statistics collected in the survey show dramatically how this influences their well-being. Forty-three per cent of those over sixty owned their own houses. This was six times as many as for people between eighteen and forty-four. It followed, therefore, that the younger group paid £10.50 a week for their family accommodation, while the elderly paid only £5.50 (these are median figures).

Another factor, more subtle, and much more fundamentally concerned with their well-being, is what people think about their own prosperity. Economics is, of course, primarily involved with the wealth – whether measured in money or by some other criterion – which people command. Whether they consider themselves to be rich or poor is, however, only partly a matter of how much material wealth they possess. It is also determined to a major degree by their expectations. Here, then, we have elderly people with a money income less than that of the non-elderly groups – who, while still in the main stream of social activity, are following them along the path leading to elderliness – yet who are better off in their housing accommodation. (The survey also showed that the food they purchased, even within the limitations of their frugal income, provided them with significantly more than the physiological demands of their bodies for nourishment.) The cool facts of the statistical tables showed that three-fifths of all the elderly had partial or complete central heating in their houses which also supplied hot water to their kitchens and bathrooms. This proportion is very much the same as that found in the homes of the people of younger ages living around them.

These are material contributions to the economic status of the elderly which, to the credit of the last two or three generations of communal kindliness, is now established, if not at a level of full equality with the workers, at least within range of equality. But the most striking contribution which the wide-ranging Age Concern research survey made to knowledge was the study which it included of the level of happiness which – regardless of money or its shortage, and health and vigour or their incompleteness – the elderly of Great Britain enjoy.

Something like two thousand people were selected as being reasonably representative of the average individual. They were sorted into groups of the eighteens to twenty-nines, the thirties to forty-fours, the forty-fives to fifty-nines and the elderly. Approval and disapproval were assessed on a numerical scale. Something rated at 0 was heartily disliked while something rated at 10 was so delightful as to be heavenly – or, as the jargon has it, fantastic. People of working age started with a built-in advantage because, in spite of the grumbling which is the tattered currency of popular chit-chat, when average people were asked to consider the matter carefully, most of them described their jobs as highly satisfactory. Yet in most aspects of life it was the elderly who scored highest in satisfaction. For example, in terms of their homes and of a whole list of the different things that might be wrong with them, it was the elderly who, it would seem, lived almost trouble-free lives while all the younger groups reported at least 50 per cent higher rates of serious disadvantages and dislikes. Whereas one-third of all the elderly people who were studied said that they could think of no way in which their houses could possibly be improved, fewer than 1 in 10 of those who were under forty-five expressed themselves as being as satisfied as that. More of the elderly liked their neighbours, and more of them enjoyed living near their friends than did younger people. Oddly enough, although for both young and old about half those investigated had relatives living in the same neighbourhood, it was the elderly who put more store on having friends living near them than at having relations near at hand.

Perhaps a more unexpected response to the enquiries about their happiness were the replies – the same in two separate studies, one done in 1973 and one in 1975 – to the question of whether they thought they needed more money than they had in order to live without worry in health and comfort. Forty per cent of the elderly replied that they did not. And well over half said that they could think of nothing they really wanted that they had to do without. On the other hand little more than a quarter of the younger half of the population were satisfied with what they had. The younger generation, even though they had, as a general rule, more money to live on, were far less contented and felt a much greater sense of privation. They, for example, believed that they would have been happier with more money to spend on holidays, washing machines, spin-driers and deep freezers, better houses in better repair, and a good car. 'These perceptions of their circumstances', wrote the survey team in their report, 'are all the more surprising since . . . the younger half of the population in fact enjoys most of these more widely than do their elders.'

In 1976, there were in Great Britain 10,784,000 people over the age of sixty, making up just under 20 per cent of the total population of 54,500,000. The elderly were made up of 6,300,000 women and 4,400,000 men. Most of these elderly people were quite well or, as it might be better to say, were as well as they used to be when they were middle aged. Even in the more restricted group of the 7,500,000 aged sixty-five and over, only 150,000 – that is, 2 per cent – had to live in institutionalized homes of one sort or another. When the elderly people were asked how happy they themselves felt about their state of health, the answers they gave were far more optimistic than many people – and particularly people who, for the most altruistic motives in the world, are struggling to make the social life of this modern industrial society better – would imagine. There are, as I discussed in chapter 2, diseases and disabilities to be overcome; there are people who live in loneliness and poverty; there are those who are unhappy and for good reason; but the fact that there are puzzling problems of medicine, economics, sociology, as well as the sorrows, misfortunes and wickedness of life, should not lead us to forget that these are, in this civilized community, minority afflictions. When the statistically selected groups of elderly people were asked to express their own degree of satisfaction about their health, the average score for all of them, men and women alike, was 7.8 (remember that 10 is perfect satisfaction, 0 utter despair); 5 therefore can be interpreted as, 'Oh, all right, I suppose', while anything better than 7 can legitimately be seen as a 'mustn't grumble!' response. But although elderly people at the time they were asked for their opinions were remarkably content with their lots, they did, when surveyed, feel that their conditions had been better when they were younger and they tended to fear that their conditions would deteriorate when they became older still. In contrast to the belief of elderly people that they were happy so far as material circumstances were concerned for the present, even though in the future (and everyone, no matter how old he or she may be, must always look forward to a future) they may be less fortunate, younger people, particularly those under forty-five, though more discontented about the present, were more optimistic about a future in which they saw themselves better off.

Finally, the diligent researchers attempted to elicit from the younger and the older groups under their scrutiny their general feelings about the usefulness of their current existence. 'Have you', they asked, 'felt during recent weeks "on top of the world?"' 'Yes', replied 44 per cent of those under forty-five. 'Yes', said 38 per cent of those between forty-five and fifty-nine. And – perhaps to the surprise of the investigators – 'yes', said an equal 38 per cent of the elderly group. On the other hand, when they were asked whether recently they had felt bored, 35 per cent of the youngest group said they had, as did 26 per cent of the middle-aged. But among the elderly, the figure was 20 per cent. Moreover, a greater number of the eighteen to forty-four-year-olds claimed periods of being 'depressed and very unhappy' (27 per cent) compared with fewer of the sixty-year-olds-and-over (21 per cent).

All, of course, is not sweetness and light. There are elderly people who are unhappy, poor and ill. Yet, in general, while we are searching for a way to make things better, it would be mistaken (and uneducated) to forget that much as already been successfully done to give many elderly people a pleasant life in the Great Britain of the times.

Just as it is not to be expected that one can obtain a precise picture of the health and happiness of any particular individual, or even of a particular category of individuals, by averaging the wealth and physical condition of the whole nation, so, too, is the picture of the elderly inevitably somewhat blurred if one averages the state of everyone over sixty. While there may be young people who are sick and unfortunate and older ones whose condition is a happy one, it is reasonable to assume that the older elderly people are more vulnerable than those who have only recently reached retirement age. With this in mind, Age Concern commissioned a study by Dr Mark Abrams in which 844 people over seventy-five (247 men and 597 women) were compared with a second group, equally carefully selected to reflect British conditions in 1977, made up of 802 people aged between sixty-five and seventy-four (315 men and 487 women).

Born around 1898, at the time of horse-drawn transport, domestic service (the occupation employing the largest number of people), before air transport, telephones or broadcasting, what vicissitudes had these older people not experienced and how radical were the social changes occurring during their lifetimes. Surely, their feelings on the state in which they found themselves in the 1970s, their opinion of the social support which the community had come to provide, and their reactions to the scientific successes, existing and potential, by which their health and vigour were protected, were worth recording.

The differences between the very old – over seventy-five – and those between sixty-five and seventy-four were not very striking. As would be expected, since women on average live so much longer, these groups consisted of more women than men, and of the over-seventy-fives who lived alone, 85 per cent were women – either widows or spinsters. On the whole, the entire group of those over seventy-five were remarkably satisfied with the way things had turned out for them. More than 80 per cent, for example, were pleased with their living quarters; two out of three were perfectly satisfied at their state of health although it is true that the remaining 30 per cent complained of a whole variety of ills, some indeed had six or seven complaints at the same time; and about half were quite satisfied with their financial status. At the two extremes of this group of older-elderly people were 14 per cent who were highly satisfied with their lot – these were the optimists – while another 14 per cent were thoroughly miserable and dissatisfied.

Even when it came to loneliness, there was no consensus. Three-quarters of those investigated received regular visits at least once a week from their families or friends. Eighty per cent of the whole group said they did not feel particularly lonely; even among those who lived alone, 70 per cent made no complaint of loneliness even when directly interrogated on the subject. Considerable efforts have been made by those with the welfare of old people at heart to set up clubs specially for their use in order to break down the isolation and ameliorate the loneliness from which, it is feared, they suffer. The study of real life coming under Dr Mark Abrams' scrutiny showed that only about one in seven of his sample of people over seventy-five were, in fact, members of clubs specially organized for their use, while another one in seven belonged to a club or organization forming part of a religious body.

To sum up briefly: as people become old and then grow older still they do become frail and infirm; nevertheless, even now, in the present state of medical science when, although much has been achieved, there is still much to be done, and at the present stage of organization which no one would admit to be perfect, the two decades from sixty to eighty can for many people be an enjoyable and useful period of life – in the future it may be made more so.

4 Choosing a Target

Apprehension is the malaise of our age. The country may, to be sure, through the knowledge and skill of its scientists and the peerless talent of its engineers, strike oil in the North Sea, but nobody throws his hat in the air and cheers. The nation is officially forbidden to be happy. We must think only of the exhaustion of resources and the consequent misery of our grandchildren deprived of what our parents never had. The luxuries and comforts of the age cannot be enjoyed with a clear conscience. The operations of the multinational companies, which combine the efforts of a consortium of once indifferent nations and increase the wealth of peoples across the world, can only be regarded with doubt, as must the consequences which we fearfully foresee of toxic hazards and disasters yet to occur. We join with Robert Burns in congratulating a field mouse on which a disaster has actually struck. 'Still art thou blest, compared wi' me!/The present only touchest thee./But, Och! I backward cast my e'e/On prospects drear!/And forward, tho' I canna see,/I guess an' fear!'

As a community, we fear being elderly; but much has been done to make old age, if not happy, at least a comfortable time of life. The road from the old poor house to the home of the modern pensioner, with his (or, more likely, her) free medicine and chiropody, with meals-on-wheels, subsidized transport and with a pension as of right, has been a long and creditable one. Yet, even though greater leisure and longer life are now available to the elderly, *happiness* cannot be guaranteed. There is a philosophical dilemma which still has to be solved: it is to do with our conception of leisure.

Leisure is a subtle idea. For the most part we construe the word leisure as the converse of work. And work, as was discussed in the last chapter, can be seen as a good or as an evil. In casual talk, work is assumed to be a hardship, something we should like to have less of – or none at all – a disagreeable necessity only undertaken provided we are paid sufficient money to do it. A moment's thought, however, demonstrates that this is a facile approach. As soon as its opposite, leisure, is given its alternative designation, unemployment, it is immediately apparent that work is for us a highly desirable thing which, in the modern technological environment in which we live, is essential to happiness. It is because elderly people have lived as members of these same technological communities for the major part of their lives before they entered the new strange era of retirement that many of them are made unhappy or, at best, bored and uneasy, by the life of leisure into which they have been thrust. Clearly, therefore, it is not enough to discuss only such matters as the health of old people, the particular illnesses and disabilities from which they may suffer and the progress being made in the scientific conquest of such conditions, nor is it sufficient to debate the adequacy of the pensions provided for them, the standard of housing and the provision of nurses, meals, transport, hearing aids and dentures – important though all these things are – if what is most potently affecting their happiness is the philosophical outlook of the community in which they live.

In the classical period of Greek civilization, from which so much of value to European culture was derived, work – or what we would dignify with the wider designation of employment – was merely a necessary activity carried out to keep the mechanism of daily life going. Free men claiming any title to culture or education, would strive to liberate themselves from the slavery of work in order to enjoy the contemplative virtues of a life of culture. When we look back at the rare periods of the flowering of civilized society, the Greek republics, the glorious and prolonged sweep of Chinese culture, the Enlightenment, the time of the Edinburgh Review, or the life of the English nobility and gentry of little more than a century ago, the target for which hardship was endured was the future enjoyment of freedom from work. In eighteenth-century England the aim was to obtain sufficient wealth to purchase a property in the country where one could live as a private gentleman without the sordid necessity of devoting one's time to labour. This tradition has remained alive to this day among privileged minorities or educated Europeans (who, in the current moral ambience, are a trifle shame-faced about it), among aristocratic families in Arabia and Persia, and, indeed, among pockets of people wherever the pervasive and dominant dogmas of the technological society have not overtaken earlier beliefs. Although this assumption – that work is merely a disagreeable preface to leisure – is at the moment unacceptable (as the modern jargon of disapproval has it) in the West, it remains a philosophical option and, as I shall later point out, may have much in its favour in the immediate future.

The Protestant ethic, born of the Reformation and supported by the dour Calvinistic tradition, was accepted so totally and unthinkingly as to be still axiomatic in our own ambiguously self-indulgent times. This tradition assumes that the primary purpose of life is work. Those who hold to this belief treat leisure as 'spare' time, that is to say, that minor part of life left over from what has been devoted to serious activity, namely, work. Even such spare time ought not to be wasted on pleasure. It should be instead used to restore and refresh people for work. It is this busy philosophy, impelling 'mad dogs and Englishmen (to) go out in the midday sun' in those indolent places which, in today's idiom, we describe as 'under-developed', and to 'develop' them. Today, the indigenous population of such lands, looking admiringly at the recent centuries of commercial expansion and industrial revolution, are themselves anxious to assume the philosophy of Western activity and develop themselves.

The interesting problem which the march of science now puts before the British citizen is that of reassessing his – or her – views on work and leisure. Gradually, but at an accelerating pace, science and the technology derived from it have led to longer holidays and shorter working weeks, to earlier retirement and a longer retired life. All this is increasing that fraction of life spent not working and reducing the time spent working without specifically altering the attitude of the community to work and leisure. What is happening to the elderly might well turn out to be a pilot run for what the community as a whole will decide to do. The question is one of choice.

Perhaps I have laboured the point already that in Great Britain it has been decided to assume that – at least for old people, whether they concur or not – work is disagreeable and leisure agreeable. In this equation, work is taken to be paid industrial or commercial employment together with such useful service activities – also paid – as school and university teaching, medicine, opera singing and politics. Leisure in this equation is, in the main, the comfortable idleness to which I have already drawn attention. The old are to be supported in comfort and warmth; their teeth, eyes and toe-nails are to be looked after, and every second Saturday bingo is to be provided at the Darby and Joan Club. Of course, to paint things thus is to imply that leisure is indeed a waste of time and to assume, as I have done in the earlier passages of this book, that the pleasant idleness of family life, even the more graceful society of the gentry as described by Jane Austen and Mrs Gaskell is not worthy of the talents and potentialities of a serious-minded person.

Up till now, and particularly since the invention of the typewriter – which was at the beginning of that so-called liberation which gave women the opportunity to choose whether (like the old-age pensioners) they wished to spend their lives comfortably, if somewhat restrictedly, supported by others, or whether they would prefer to embrace the liberty provided by the money they earned and to enjoy the social variety of the factory and the typing pool – the modern choice has been that work is good and idleness bad. The main hardship for the elderly is to find themselves compelled to accept the alternative proposition. Before we consider how to overcome this hardship – as, for so many, hardship it is – and how to work towards the implementation of a Fair Employment Act for the elderly, it would perhaps be useful to consider whether there is evidence to suggest that this present age of the idealization of work may be coming to an end.

In trying to forecast change in generally accepted social assumptions, it may be of limited value to interrogate ordinary people. At the time when the tower-block apartments for working-class families were being built, everyone was agreed that this was an enterprising and forward-looking application of technology to the problem of the slums. Today, no one has a word to say in favour of tall towers. When Marie Stopes first publicly mooted the social virtues of the use of mechanical contraceptives for 'family planning', she was met with massive disapproval. Today the virtues of such technology are as overwhelmingly applauded. Both these changes in social attitudes took place, almost as do changes in women's fashions or popular music, as if of themselves. In our community it has been held that, for the young and the middle-aged work is good and excessive leisure is bad – but for the elderly the reverse applies. As a community, is this an issue on which we are going to change our collective mind?

In a recent book,* Bernard D Nossiter, London correspondent of the Washington Post, has reached the conclusion that the people of Great Britain are already doing so. His observations fall into two categories. The first implies that when they *are* working, the British have decided that they do not choose to work so frantically as the Japanese, the Germans or the Americans. Instead, they take things easy, break off from work to enjoy cups of tea, and are prepared to make do with a smaller number of the more advanced technological products than communities for whom work is accepted as a self-evident good enjoy. On the other hand, according to Bernard Nossiter, the British when they *do* work are turning away from heavy engineering, mining and the manufacture of useful objects such as motor-cars and machine tools and devoting their attention increasingly to things of the mind and spirit.

As evidence in support of his thesis, Nossiter cites one of Great Britain's biggest enterpreneurs, Lord Cowdray, who has gradually redeployed his resources so that, in place of the production of material goods, his operations cover the merchant bank, Lazard Brothers; the publication of ideas, stories and thoughts through his ownership of Penguin Books; the influencing of current affairs and the economy through the possession of the Financial Times, a daily paper that not only deals with finance but which has achieved remarkable popular success through its literary excellence; the production of elegant china through ownership of the long established works of Royal Doulton; and further extension into things of the mind through the ownership of a series of local news-

* *A Future that Works*, Bernard D. Nossiter, André Deutsch, 1978.

papers in Great Britain and of a leading American publishing house, Viking Press. Perhaps Nossiter's point is most strikingly illustrated by the ownership by the Cowdray people of Madam Tussauds, a waxwork show which is one of the country's most popular tourist attractions, and Warwick Castle, one of the most beautiful and romantic of the nation's historic treasures. The development of the argument implies that there may be a limit to the extent to which a perceptive community is prepared to expend the energy of its members on the manufacture of articles of utility and luxury by day and their utilization by night. If Nossiter is right, it would imply that a change is taking place in the social assumptions of the community. Such change could lead to a situation in the future in which 'absenteeism' would be welcomed rather than deplored, and we should find that steps would be taken to arrange for it on a systematic basis. Nossiter's second point is that, while moving from the devotion of attention to the manufacture of material things – steel, sulphuric acid and textiles – towards more cerebral and artistic products such as banking services, books, scenery and wax images of memorable men and women, the British community is well maintaining a sufficient level of material prosperity. Although the absolute wealth of the nation per head of its citizens may not be as great as that of the harder-working societies, the relative rate of improvement in economic status and the agreeability of life are fully comparable.

This kind of change in social thinking, if indeed it is happening, would seem rational in the light of the abrupt and rapid advance in science leading to the development of very small transistor units which are enabling specialized computers to be produced cheaply and in a form enabling them to be built into mechanical control units of all sorts. This process of so-called miniaturization, based on these tiny transistors combined into silicon 'chips', is already making it possible to do with automatic machinery a wide variety of things for which human labour was previously required. This is true for operations ranging from manufacturing processes to type-setting in printing works, from stock keeping and invoicing in retail shops to the sorting of letters in post offices – indeed, paper, ink, envelopes and stamps are no longer necessary to convey messages at all! Clearly, it would be a happy eventuality if the British community found itself actually enjoying leisure and accepting work, if as a burden at all, at least as one to be cheerfully accepted, just at a period in history when ordinary life – and one of comfort and prosperity – came to consist mainly of leisure. Such a change of attitude, if it did come, would immediately ameliorate the state of the elderly who would then no longer find themselves divorced from the rest of the community by the basic assumptions governing the lives of their fellows.

Nossiter's predictions may be overstated and his argument that an advanced society such as that of Great Britain could be economically sustained with very much reduced primary industry and by a much greater concentration on service activities and intellectual and artistic enterprises may not prove feasible to the degree he forecasts. Nevertheless, even if the real balance of work may change little, a change in attitude is certainly not to be ruled out. 'There is nothing good or bad, but thinking makes it so,' said Shakespeare. Not long ago, a community thought it good that an oil refinery or a steel works should be set up nearby. Would this not make employment – that essential constituent of a happy life – more readily available? Suddenly, however, a change in thinking occurred. Today, any proposal to build a power station or plastics factory, no matter how much the people need electricity or hanker after nylon, has the local community up in arms and the government itself, reflecting the public emotion, will demand an 'environmental impact' enquiry. If a parallel change in the public attitude to what constitutes a good life should take place, different views of work and leisure could come to be equally widely accepted. It is for society to choose.

But while in Great Britain where, in spite of constant admonitions to work harder, strike less capriciously, and increase output, there is some evidence for thinking that a view may be gaining ground which could lead to a general acceptance that contentment may be attainable without having to hold employment as the highest good, there is yet another choice open. In the United States, where the genius of the nation attaches particular importance to two principles of social behaviour, namely, devotion to a clearly understandable and legally enforceable written constitution on the one hand and a traditional admiration for financial success based on commercial and industrial endeavour on the other, a different approach is apparent. The American community, it could be argued, is making the alternative choice and, as its fundamental philosophy, may decide that to be employed in economically-rewarded work is a basic right of which no citizen shall be arbitrarily deprived.

The first major step in this direction was the passing in 1967 of the Age Discrimination in Employment Act. This arose from the Civil Rights Act of 1964 which directed the Secretary of Labour of that time, Mr W. Willard Wirtz, to draw up a report to show the degree to which people who were in their forties, fifties and sixties, and therefore no longer young, suffered from discrimination in employment on account of their age. This report showed that as men and women in America grew older it became increasingly difficult for them to get jobs. For example, in thirteen States where there were no laws about age, 25 per cent of applicants over forty-five found themselves excluded because of their age, while virtually no one over fifty-five could usefully apply at all.

Even though the Act of 1967 made it illegal to discriminate against people applying for work on account of their age, a powerful ground swell of opinion appears to be carrying the matter further. The act only applies to those up to the age of sixty-five, leaving older people unaffected and, according to Robert Butler, in his powerful and savage book published in 1975,* it is often circumvented and not applied in cases where it might be. Butler, indeed, details a number of them and lists the sums, in millions of dollars, which groups of successful litigants have been awarded.

The argument that has been developed in the United States, that work is the highest form of pleasure and that people should not be deprived of work merely because they are old, is a powerful one. The conclusions of university research support the belief that money is one of the major pleasures resulting from work – regardless of what the money is spent on – and is intimately involved with happiness, self-esteem and social adjustment. If this is the case, a further conclusion which may be drawn is that voluntary social work which is done without pay cannot be a substitute for 'real' work done for money. And it also follows by the same argument that golf, shuffleboard and other forms of time-filling which, up till now, 'senior citizens' have been encouraged to take part in may not, in fact, be a satisfactory culmination to a busy life. It is even being said that the colonies for elderly people with their specially built dwellings surrounded by suitably landscaped acres in Florida, California, and other places scattered about the United States where the weather is good, may, regardless of their carefully thought-out arrangements, technical, social and financial, fail to make life worthwhile for those who live in them but merely provide – in the telling American phrase – 'play-pens for the old'.

* *Why Survive?*, Robert Butler, Harper and Row (New York), 1975.

In recent years there have been leaders among those Americans who believe in the primacy of work for all – even the elderly – who have been campaigning against the mortal sin of 'agism'. It is only with the last short generation that of all the sins, 'racism' – the deprivation of a person's right and privileges on account of race – has come to be regarded as the most heinous. 'Agism', the sin of discriminating against any citizen on account of age, is now a sin of equal turpitude. It is in the light of this philosophy that the Discrimination in Employment Act, which specifically excluded people over sixty-five, is so palpably unsatisfactory. And besides the moral compulsion not to deny the elderly the satisfaction of paid employment, there is also – it now seems – a medical reason for continuing paid industrial employment among the elderly indefinitely.

Butler refers to a number of studies, the implications of which, it would seem, are to show that, having supported themselves by work all their lives and been themselves supported by work, as the central meaning, purpose and joy of their existence, people become 'workaholics'. This is not a disease, as its etymology would imply, but the proper state of fitness of adult members of the industrial community. When, so the clinical evidence apparently shows, the supporting influence of work is removed from the elderly withdrawal symptoms occur. These have been particularized by those who have made a study of the problem in America as anxiety and depression, headache, nervousness and tension, gastroenteritis, over-sleeping, lethargy and irritability. The whole thing has been described as the 'retirement syndrome'.

Perhaps there is a difference between what can sensibly be called a disease for which a medical remedy can be prescribed and the more generalized unease to which Shakespeare, for example, refers when he asks 'who can minister to a mind diseased?' The significant point is, however, that the philosophical outlook behind the American diagnosis could be taken to be the assumption that work is a beneficial therepeutic activity and that no citizen should be deprived of it against his will. Acting upon this presupposition, Professor John Weiss brought an action in 1970 against the governors of Fordham University for preventing his taking up the position of Albert Schweitzer Professor of Philosophy, to which he had been appointed, on the grounds that, because he was sixty-nine years of age, he was too old. He claimed in the US District Court that the Older Americans Act of 1965 lays on the government of the United States the duty 'to secure equal opportunity to the full and free enjoyment of ... employment with no discriminating personnel practices because of age'. He lost his case, the judge ruling, firstly, that in the end abilities do diminish with age and, secondly, that retirement was not discriminatory if it applied to everyone who lived the requisite number of years.

The momentum of the philosophical presupposition acted upon by John Weiss is gaining ground at every level of the American governmental and legal systems. Pressures are being applied to industry, to the civil service, even to the army, to support the thesis that, work being a good and desirable thing, employers hiring men and women must be just as little biased by their age as by their colour. Organizations representing the old have been formed in the United States in order to concentrate powerful political influence to ensure, among other aims, that the government enforces the right of elderly people to work. The National Council on the Aging started in 1945 with a voluntary staff of one. By 1973, its paid staff numbered 106, it had 10 regional offices and a budget of three-and-a-half million dollars. Another organization, The Consultation of Older and Younger Adults, numbering its members in thousands, has, through its political and extra-political activities, acquired for its adherents the title of the Gray Panthers. Then there are the Retired Professional Action Group and the National Caucus of the Black Aged also exercising political muscle.

The American influence in international combinations of old people is strong. The International Senior Citizens Association, founded initially – although one would not have thought so in view of its name – in Copenhagen, now has its headquarters in Los Angeles. The International Federation on Aging is based in Washington DC. Robert Butler is now proposing the formation of a council for national organizations of the elderly, while Senator Church seeks to activate the United Nations to mobilize a World Assembly on Aging. Among the variety of aims towards which the efforts of all these bodies should be directed, Butler lists in his 'Agenda for Activism' the setting up of employment agencies to find jobs for the elderly, and the creation of organizations to support right-to-work suits: encouraging refusal to leave jobs on compulsory retirement and enforcing such refusal by arranging for 'sit-ins' at the place of work.

The kind of life lived by elderly citizens in the Soviet Union reveals a philosophical outlook remarkably similar to the one which, it seems, is becoming widespread in the United States. These great republics, both born out of revolution and struggle, and both dependent for their power and strength on subduing a wilderness and bringing it under cultivation for the ultimate benefit of its citizens, hold work in high esteem. But, whereas in the United States policy evolves from the competing pressures of combinations of individuals, in the Soviet Union, within the broad philosophical framework of socialism, it is established by central authority. According to R. C. Revutskaya, the chief of the Operation Research Unit at the Institute of Gerontology in Kief,* what is done for old people in the Soviet Union is

* *Geriatric Care in Advanced Societies*, ed. J. C. Brocklehurst, MTB, 1975.

designed 'to allow older people wherever possible to remain in their normal environment, to prolong their working period and to preserve mobility and the ability for self-service. A good psychic state keeps up their full social competence.' The last sentence, as I have argued earlier, is the important one. Having lived all their adult lives in a community where work – rightly or wrongly – is held in the highest esteem, the elderly people are not expected to have to adapt themselves to an existence in which work plays no part and leisure, a state of nothingness in which, obviously, neither the cultivation of aristocratic pursuits nor devotion to religious contemplation could be countenanced, is all that remains.

In order to keep the elderly fit for work as long as possible, the Soviet authorities encourage them to join 'Groups of Health'. These are units set up all over the USSR in sports clubs, physical-training 'dispensaries', medical institutes and other places. Elderly members of 'Groups of Health' are put through a programme of physical training grounded on physiological principles and graded according to the age and physique of the elderly individual concerned. The Groups have become, in Dr Revutskaya's words, 'mass physico-cultural keep-fit institutions for the aged'.

A parallel scheme to restore the working capacity of elderly people which advancing age is beginning to sap, and otherwise to prolong the productive and active period of their lives, is the institution of Health Zones. These establishments may be set up in a municipal park or elsewhere in the cities where the elderly people live. A Health Zone will have in it facilities for gymnastics and other exercises, a dining room where what Dr Revutskaya describes as 'dietary nourishment' is provided, accommodation for medical examinations, and pavilions where those attending the courses can sit down and rest when their programme of activities calls for a rest period. Elderly people attend a Health Zone for a course lasting from forty to sixty days. The programme they go through is intended to combine regular activities, exercises and gymnastics suited to their capacity as determined by a preliminary medical examination, and work therapy. As a general rule, drugs are not used but each day those attending the Health Zone are tuned up by physical training, supervised walking, by sports of various kinds and 'hydrotherapy'. At Pyatigorsk, to give one example, the Zone is in the Park of Culture and Rest; the programme is planned and carried out under the supervision of volunteer pensioners and the physical exercises are organized by a medical gymnast.

While the main function of the Groups of Health and the Health Zones, based on the assumption that the purpose of existence is work, is to prolong the working life of Soviet citizens, it is interesting to note that provision is also made for the time when people are no longer able to work. The programme of activities can be modified so as to allow time for diversion. Reading, knitting and sewing are mentioned as examples of such recreations, and the work-therapy part of the programme of rehabilitation can be appropriately modified for those who have grown too old for industrial employment so that the time formerly devoted to it is filled with what are intended to be useful, meaningful occupations. For those who have accepted work as the primary function of their adult existence, we could well imagine that such a provision when they are old might constitute a less disturbing choice than the shuffleboard and golf of a different culture.

All advanced societies, whether that of the United States or the Soviet Union, or the Netherlands or Great Britain, finding themselves abruptly faced with the comparatively new and unexpected problem of the elderly, have stumbled to a greater or a lesser degree into the same philosophical ambiguity. All such societies have in practice come to accept work as the main purpose of life. Full employment is the goal of every

national policy. In the Soviet Union virtual full employment has apparently been achieved, and the happiness
of the citizenry (or at least their reasonable satisfaction at
having a job) is continued as long as possible into old
age. The ambiguity, so much more apparent in non-
socialist countries, of calling on the elderly to sever their
ties with the working population, of which they have so
long been members, and live in uneasy idleness, or shall
we say leisure, is thereby reduced to a minimum. In the
United States too, where work is held in as high esteem
as it is by the Soviets, now that the retirement compul-
sions are gradually being eroded, it will soon be possible
for the elderly to remain in employment if they wish – as
many of them no doubt will – until the end of their lives.

In Great Britain, the philosophical outlook and the
public will are less decided. While it is difficult to
dissent from the popular wisdom of the times – everyone
has to be in favour of democracy, unisex and wild life,
and against capital punishment, smoking and the parade
of luxury – there is a minority of people who have never
abandoned the unfashionable aristocratic notion that
work, when it is necessary at all, is merely an irksome
prelude to a more rewarding, leisured existence dedi-
cated to the pursuit of higher ends. And added to these
there may be – as Nossiter foresees – a growing number
of people who are coming to enjoy the freedom of spirit
that leisure brings, even if those in authority call such
leisure absenteeism.

Political leaders, whether of the left or of the right, are
united in accepting the assumption that work is the
salvation of society and that leisure is reprehensible. In
the early days of the North American republic, the
philosophy of Jefferson held that through work men and
women would obtain a better life for themselves and be
freed from dependence on others. Long after the justification to work hard to produce enough to keep the
population fed, clothed and housed had been under-

mined by the outpouring of goods by machines, the population was still urged to make new efforts in order to enjoy the fruits of the consumption economy of throw-away objects – from disposable underclothes to continually modified motor cars. One of the underlying motives behind the stridency of the present movement for women's liberation is the great reservoir of moral conviction according to which idleness is equated with moral turpitude. Nor does idleness, as the word is used in this sense, imply a supine abandonment to doing nothing. Housewives may work hard for long hours but since they are not employed for wages their activities count little for virtue.

There is little hope that the public mind will soon change its traditional way of thinking, old fashioned though it can every year more palpably be seen to be. Socialist leaders decry the idle rich as parasites on the backs of the workers. Capitalist politicians bemoan the moral decay of lazy workers. Yet on every hand, the productivity of science-based technology which, as exemplified in medicine, has brought the elderly into being as a major social group, is in offices, factories, schools, in typesetting, banking, manufacture and agriculture rapidly reducing the need for human participation.

If the ordinary citizen believes that only through paid employment is the good life to be attained, the elderly citizen will believe the same. Is he not the same man he was a few years earlier? And if the ordinary man's belief is mistaken, if in fact the actual work he does (apart fom its adventitious social meaning) is trivial and degrading, then his efforts on behalf of the elderly, if they succeed – and succeed they will – will be mistaken too.

In considering what is the wise and proper condition of the elderly, to the attainment of which our efforts should be directed, it is obviously important to consider at the same time what is the proper goal of ordinary

citizens who are not elderly. The choice of target is not
the blunt selection of leisure or work – one or the other.
To start with, before choosing either, both must be
defined. There are those for whom their work, if it
cannot exactly be categorized as leisure, is undoubtedly
something very close to pleasure. Nor is the definition of
leisure altogether easy to make. A man or woman whose
hobby is politics, may end up as an elected member of a
local authority and may be found attending meetings late
into the night, six days a week, quite apart from having
to read papers and listen interminably to the troubles of
constituents. Is all this leisure?

What then is the wise choice and who is to set the
criteria by which it is to be made? The prophet, the
man or woman with the insight to stand up and speak for
what is excellent and worthwhile, who has seen it all and
has nothing to lose, may be the one who will first urge
the elderly to wake up to their opportunity and they, by
choosing well themselves, may set the target for the
entire community. Men and women in their sixties, who
can expect to be in full possession of their health and
their intellectual faculties, provided by the community
with a private income, modest, to be sure, but sufficient
for people of judgment, can lead their fellows towards a
worthwhile leisured life. This need not be a life of
idleness, neither need it be an extension of the unexciting grind of the shop floor or the office. Indeed, this kind
of occupation may well, within a generation, become a
thing of the past.

One way in which this philosophy, which perhaps
appears romantic and sentimental to present thinking,
may take the place of the current yearning for employment before retirement and resigned frustration not
unmixed with self-pity after it, may well be the accession
to the growing ranks of the retired of younger and
younger recruits. This will happen if the active trend in
America towards the insistence of the elderly on what

they almost assume to be a principle of human rights – to stay in the factories in their old age, is mirrored by the opposite trend in Great Britain – to retire earlier and often to retire with a considerable capital sum, if the arrangement can be made to fall within the arbitrary definition of 'redundancy'. Once there arises within the group of the elderly (who, like American 'veterans', need not in fact be particularly old) the single man or woman prepared to raise the banner of excellence, either in polite manners and good behaviour or in the pursuit of some good thing for its own sake, then the goal of a life of leisure, which the enormous ability of technology to produce wealth makes possible, could more quickly than we think come to be accepted by the whole community as a worthy one.

Some years ago, George Woodcock, sometime General Secretary of the Trades Union Congress, was talking on the radio about his boyhood. He spoke of his parents, self-reliant working people in the mould of the earnest, radical proletariat of the past, fighting for freedom and recognition of the rights of man. At that time the Workers Educational Association was held in high esteem. It provided a means by which labourers could receive some education, learn to speak in grammatical straightforward sentences and so gain control of their own destiny. As Woodcock reminded his radio audience, in those days, it would have been a disgrace to boast of roistering over a wilderness of beer shouting catcalls at a stripper exposing her nakedness to a roomful of men claiming leadership of the community. At that time the purpose of life and the never-ending struggle which, no matter how wealthy a nation may become, is always an inherent part of the human condition was epitomized in the Workers' Catechism. Unattached to official religion and the convoluted dogmas of the established churches, this called for loyalty, steadfastness and sacrifice for the good of others, especially those suffering misfortune.

Now that the work ethic can be seen to be insufficient, so productive has modern technology proved itself to be, and the failure of material possessions – of package holidays in Spain, of colour television sets and 'music centres' – to bring happiness is generally apparent, an earlier and more satisfying target will be chosen in its place.

Excellence can take a number of forms. In present-day Britain there are quite a large number of young men and women setting themselves up as photographers and struggling to succeed; even so, publicity managers and advertising agents complain of a shortage of creative photographers. For every 'pop' group that has attracted attention, there are scores of others striving in their own way to excel. Television repair men, plumbers, decorators, clock menders and piano tuners – all of whom have succeeded in doing what the rest of us are not able to do – are to be found living their own lives. Are their pursuits work or leisure?

Should there evolve a middle way, in which what people chose to do in their leisure merged with what they did when they considered themselves to be at work, the elderly, in receipt of the pension which gives them freedom to choose (admittedly within the constraints of what we must hope to be a humane community), could themselves merge with the rest of their fellows and, by doing so, resolve the main cause of their discontent today.

5 Half-way House

Whatever may happen in the future to homogenize the population and knit the elderly into the warm and active fabric of society, a number of interesting developments are to be seen at the present time. One of particular promise is Link Opportunity. The interesting notions behind this imaginative conception are, firstly, that it is intended to provide for elderly people real work suited to the particular talents and abilities of each. It takes cognizance, however, of the fact that in a well organized society the elderly can be expected to be in receipt of a personal private income, namely, their pension, and each individual can therefore work as much or as little as he or she chooses. Most important of all, the scheme has done away with altruism. Those who need work done for them expect to pay for it. This they are able to do either by a system of direct barter, that is to say, by doing work for the person who has done work for them or, as is more likely to happen, by the use of units of a special currency, which constitutes an essential part of the scheme. The backing for each unit of this currency is an hour's work by a member of the scheme. It does not matter what kind of work it is. It may be typing, house-cleaning, carpentry, working in the office which forms the centre of each geographical unit into which the scheme is divided, or serving as a salesman for the plants grown in a Link garden centre, should there be one.

An early centre of Link Opportunity was set up by Edward Walton in the large and socially diverse borough of Brent in London, with, at the start, half a dozen telephone-answering machines. It was publicized, initially, by the distribution of leaflets in the street, by information broadcasts on the local radio station and by such other means as came to hand. Those who were interested in joining identified themselves, described their particular qualifications, which could be domestic arts such as cooking, washing, cleaning or sewing; technical skills; or academic or professional attainments. A diffident elderly woman who, in the existing ambience of retirement, was doubtful about the effectiveness of her talents but who quickly proved herself to possess outstanding administrative ability, soon took over the central office. There, by the straightforward means of hanging coloured labels on to pins stuck into a map of the district, she and others who came later to join the enterprise, fixed the location of all those who volunteered their diverse skills. Before long, they were able to match those who were anxious to make use of what they could do with those who wanted something done. These, too, telephoned, wrote or paid the centre a visit. Their names and needs were also set down on labels of the appropriate colour and pinned up on the map so that the matching of needs to offers could be conveniently done. Soon there were people putting up shelves, turning the cuffs and collars of shirts, filling in statutory forms received from the Council office for those unable to comprehend them, cleaning and restarting the grandfather clock – and receiving for each hour's work a unit of currency, in form not dissimilar from a trading stamp, to add to the initial subvention of currency which every member of the scheme was given on joining.

The benefits of the Link Opportunity idea are manifold as a half-way provision which the elderly can supply for themselves while those who are not elderly still view industrial employment as the primary goal of life. The first benefit is the outlet it provides for the energy and skill of its members. The second benefit is that of enriching the social life of those who take part in it. Whether they like or dislike the member of the Link scheme who has come to put a new plug on the toaster, whether the unexpected complexity of sorting out the entries needed to obtain the remittance of income tax due to the garrulous widow is likely to make the member who is a retired income-tax inspector late for his next appointment or not, all of those involved must be enriching their experience if, before they joined the scheme, they had no outlet for their energies at all. The third benefit that such an arrangement as Link Opportunity provides is that, while it is not geared directly into the fiscal machinery of the community, the artificial money on which it operates does possess real economic value. For example, if the life of a shirt is extended by half by having its collar and cuffs turned, an operation capable of being carried out in an hour by a skilled worker, the value of the unit of currency involved is equal to half the price of a shirt. There is no need to point out the economic value, measured in terms of plumbers' and electricians' bills, of the work done by a Link Exchange member capable of replacing tap washers or electric fuses.

While doubtless an improvement on bingo and cups of tea, it can be argued that the constructive quality of the work undertaken by Link members cannot always pretend to be particularly absorbing. Here and there, however, possibilities for the fundamental development of the Link scheme emerge. A Link Exchange operating in the London suburb of Merton received a visit from a quite different group in nearby Walton and Weybridge. This group had been organized for the mutual support of widows and widowers and, indeed, of anyone faced with the task of bringing up children alone. Such people find themselves presented with peculiar difficulties, as does the group comprising the elderly. For both, there are special problems relating to the maintenance of a place within the main working stream of the community in which they live. It was, therefore, interesting to find that the two groups readily combined to their mutual advantage. The Link members who could sew found eager demand for their services from the group responsible for children, while the latter group could cook and, on occasion, drive for the elderly Link members.

With all its limitations, the ingenious Link scheme demonstrates that, if there is the energy and the administrative talent available, elderly people can organize themselves into a social unit through which, while enjoying the leisure of retirement, they can at the same time be involved in meaningful social activity. Most interesting of all is the demonstration that such a group – everyday people enjoying both employment and leisure – can establish a worthwhile arrangement with a quite different group, also alienated from the main stream of social life.

Much of the scholarly writing about old age today, a good deal of which has been done in the United States, is written as sociology or social history. For example D. H. Fischer, in his excellent book *Growing Old in America*,* describes his purpose in writing it as, firstly, to establish the main lines of change over the short two hundred years of American history; secondly, to dig information out of the archives prepared for quite other purposes; and, finally, to make a coherent narrative out of what is available and thus recognize the relation of the present to the past. But it is surely also possible to view the present in relation to the past with the idea of doing something about it. We know that modern society is stratified; that children constitute one category, subdivided into pre-school children, school children and

---

* *Growing Old in America*, D. H. Fischer, Oxford University Press (New York), 1977.

students; that adults are separately grouped into workers, housewives, the retired elderly, and a certain number of fringe groups; but history shows us that something *can* be done to change the trends of the time. And with the private income of the elderly gradually coming to them at an earlier age, while at the same time eligibility for the private income of the young (sometimes called a student grant or a subvention for a retraining scheme) is being extended to include people of more and more advanced years, the need for real and creative activity regardless of what isolated stratum of the community an individual belongs to is becoming increasingly important. If we were sufficiently ingenious, it would already be possible – so efficient are modern automated and computerized production techniques – for the majority of the population to be granted a private pension to allow them, should they so wish, to enjoy a life of leisure in which their time would be at their own disposal. I shall discuss some of the problems involved in such an eventuality in the next chapter.

Meanwhile it is useful to examine what it is that elderly people, still capable, and within the ages of, say, sixty and eighty, choose to do at the present time. It must of course be recognized that the uniform policies imposed by the large-scale organizations of modern society, whether such organizations are unions or large companies, the State itself as represented by the civil service, or even the church, very seldom allow the elderly the luxury of choice.

There are two activities which, within at least this half of the century, have been dwindling in importance as opportunities for employment. One is farming and the other shopkeeping. Yet both have continued to offer scope for those of the elderly who desire to remain within the corpus of the community, and enable them to enjoy the knowledge that they are continuing to make a useful contribution to that community. Although the

march forward of technological progress has revolution-
ized agriculture and is rapidly doing the same to the
retail trade (there is already a hypermarket operating in
the north of England where the customer, pushing the
goods he or she has collected on a trolly through an elec-
tronically scrutinized gate, can have his or her bank
account debited, by way of an appropriate credit card,
without currency or people being involved), a niche
remains in both for elderly workers. Old farm labourers,
and the old lady who operates a sweet shop or supervises
the sale of knitting wool and patterns, can both continue
satisfactorily to an advanced age. It is interesting to
speculate that the reason for this is that both farming and
shopkeeping involve contact with living creatures. Could
it be that the change which I foresee might be an
encouragement of these trends, when once it becomes
recognized that, however richly endowed with advanced
technology it might be, a good society is one which is
tender both to animals and to people?

There are, of course, elderly people who enjoy the
relaxation of retirement as it is now after a long life of
labour. It is difficult to assess how many of these there
are. To start with, many of those interrogated in such
surveys as have been done may have expressed themselves as satisfied from a simple desire not to appear dissatisfied when questioned by a member of a survey team.
There is another reason as well. The head of an employment agency for elderly people to whom I was speaking observed that a comparatively short time after having
been compulsorily retired, those who initially regretted
having been steered into a social backwater were so
deeply affected by the trauma of retirement that they fell
into a state of supine resignation. This group, however,
should be contrasted with those others who react differently and for whom the boredom and emptiness of the
life they find themselves living – cultured and civilized
leisure having escaped them – act as spurs to their efforts

to find a useful outlet for their energies. The tally, so far as it was assessed by Age Concern in 1971 in an estimate based on a study of 42,000 pensioners in the London borough of Southwark, was that, of these, 13 per cent were sufficiently anxious to find work to feel impelled to actively seek employment.

Whereas the Link Opportunity idea which we have already discussed aims to operate as a co-operative scheme in which what its members do depends on what its other members want done and is, therefore, a self-sustaining operation within the community of the elderly, there have been other operations designed to keep the elderly within the main stream of the community as a whole. For example, in Glasgow, a 'Part-time Employment Bureau for the Retired' was set up by the Glasgow Retirement Council. Operating from a rent-free office, provided with free typing, postage and telephone, and making no charge for its services, the Bureau was staffed by a team of voluntary interviewers. Out of the first batch of 2,600 elderly men who came in search of employment, 730, that is nearly a third, were found part-time jobs. These were mainly in shops, offices and garages. While many of the applicants were working men who had previously been employed in comparatively unskilled jobs, some of them had held executive positions. Rather to the surprise of the people running the Bureau, these were often quite pleased to be given simple work, for example, filing in a solicitor's office, despatching the mail or running errands, often for a half day, from one o'clock until half past five in the afternoon. They were pleased to have an occupation free from the worry of responsibility. When elderly women who had previously done clerical work applied, little difficulty was encountered in fixing them up with work of the same kind. Now a total of 2,700 people aged sixty-five and over have been found part-time jobs and that is 50 per cent of all who applied.

Again it could be argued that this was a half-way operation. The initiative came from voluntary effort, the jobs
were found in the main by personal contact with Rotary
Clubs and Chambers of Commerce and the work was
part-time. One reason for this was the pernicious tax system whereby any earnings higher that what, in terms of
the real world of work, was a trivial amount were
deducted from the elderly worker's pension – a penalty
intended to be, as indeed it is, highly discouraging to
anyone wishing to continue work after compulsory
retirement. A curious and unexpected outcome of this
penal enactment was that on a number of occasions
when there were vacancies for full-time or relief night-
watchmen, these were filled by candidates seventy years
old or older, at which age this fiscal penalty ceases to
apply.

There are schemes similar to the Part-time Employment Bureau in other parts of Great Britain, The Elderly
Project, Southwark, in London is one. It is in touch with
social workers employed by the Local Authority, with
doctors and hospitals who may feel that some of their
elderly patients would be better off if they were at work,
and with business men's clubs and associations. In this
scheme the potential workers were recruited from places
where pensioners congregate, such as luncheon clubs
and day centres. Not all of the applicants, even though
they thought that they would like to be back at work,
found that they were up to it when they were put to the
test. It would seem that the sedative influence of retirement, compounded of what the general community
thought about the fitness of the elderly for anything
other than playing bingo and taking the dog for a walk,
and what the elderly thought about themselves, had
already taken effect. In particular, the old people of
Southwark felt themselves enmeshed in the web of regulations governing pensions, earning rights, rate rebates,
income tax and supplementary benefits to such a degree

that they were timorous of disturbing the complexity underlying the weekly payments made to them by the face behind the post office grill, who so obviously knew better than they what to give to them each week. While employment was provided for some of the elderly men as part-time cleaners, messengers, doormen, handymen in warehouses and stores – and a man with a law degree was found a job in a bookshop – and while women gained employment as cleaners, in clerical work, a few as shop assistants and a few more as semi-skilled workers in factories, a significant proportion of the time of the Bureau was occupied in reassuring applicants, whether they ever went to work or not, about their pension rights, and all the complex enactments which benevolent authorities had, at one time or another, promulgated for their benefit and, it must be said, to their alarm and bewilderment as well.

There are, here and there, even in the current social ambience which sees the elderly as sitting quietly on park benches – when the public eye ever does focus in a philosophical way on their condition at all – indications that they could still be capable of making a real contribution to the working life of the community. A significant phenomenon of modern life has been the growth of employment consultants. A company proposing to establish a branch factory on Merseyside, in Scotland, or in a regenerated cotton town in the north of England may well employ a consulting firm to recruit, not only the skilled technical and managerial staff who will be needed, but everybody else as well. One, at least, of such firms found that among the diverse people of varied ages and qualifications who passed through their hands, were a sprinkling of elderly men and women. After all, if Harold Macmillan in his eighties can effectively continue as chairman of a great publishing firm, why should not less distinguished people hope to make their contributions at less exalted levels? Be that as it may, the employment

consultants to whom I refer, sensing, as good business-
men should, that here was a profitable area of endeavour,
set up, as part of their diversified group of specialist
agencies a subsidiary company which was an employment agency for people over sixty.

In 1977 they carried out a survey of 880 of the elderly
people who had passed through their hands in London
and nearby, and in Manchester. Of these, 566 were men
and 314 women. This group, inevitably self-selected,
being people who had taken active steps to find themselves work, were predominantly individuals who had
been involved in office or commercial work. Whether the
great body of industrial workers were only too pleased to
stop doing it or, having lived their working lives in an
environment where it was assumed that decisions were
always to be taken *en masse* rather than individually, they
had no thought of moving out of the state of retirement
in which they found themselves, there is no evidence to
show. Most of the elderly workers in the survey, besides
being men – the predominance was particularly marked
in Manchester – were also in possession of a living wife
(or husband). Again we do not know whether it was the
encouragement of a spouse which contributed to the
enterprise and vigour of the elderly workers, or whether
the feeling of being in the way when at home and neg-
lectful of the other when abroad on pleasure provided the
spur to seek employment. In London it was found that
more of the elderly people who worked, worked full time,
and more of them (about half) worked at what they had
done in earlier life than those elsewhere. For example, in
Manchester, only 10 per cent were found to continue in
their retirement job what they had done before; the other
90 per cent did something quite different. An explana-
tion for these two phenomena could be that the cost of
living in London, including the cost of travelling to
work – travel concessions for the elderly specifically prevent their making use of them at working times – is so

high that elderly workers feel impelled to do what will bring in most money.

When the people investigated by the employment agency were asked how long they would like to continue working, given the opportunity to do so, more than half of those in Manchester and other places outside London said that they would like to go on doing so indefinitely. In London, the proportions of those who said that they wanted to go on working for ever was about a third. Most of those answering these questions were, however, in their sixties and there is, of course, no knowing what their answers would have been as they grew older and more infirm. It should be noted that the agency success-fully filled a vacancy for an invoice typist with a candi-date of eighty-two. Undoubtedly, there are substantial numbers of elderly people who would like to go on work-ing much longer than the rigid system of retirement, originally evolved for their comfort and protection, allows. As the system works at present, it is somewhat paradoxical to find that outside London, where the prop-ortion of people wanting to stay at work is larger, retire-ment is mainly between fifty-five and sixty, whereas in London, where the proportion of those anxious to work on is lower, retirement tends to be between sixty and sixty-five.

The purpose of the complex social life which we now live in our present technological age is not something that ordinary people find easy to define. When a travel-ler visits Switzerland, he finds admirable many aspects of the life of the Swiss. The railway system is marvellously punctual and the national air line reliable. Diverse nationalities live together in political calm. The Japan-ese, like the Swiss, live in a geographical environment providing few natural resources to contribute to the wealth which they, with such peerless intellectual energy, combine together to produce. Widely different in race, history, tradition and religion, it is not easy to see the social goal for which either of these peoples strive. And what do the British strive for? When the elderly candidates for employment in and around London and in Manchester were asked why they wanted to work, top of the list of their priorities came money, and next came the need of something to do and someone to tell them to do it. Last reason of all was the pleasure to be gained from conversation with the other rowers as, together, they gently propel the ship of state towards that obscure destination of which the shadows are gradually becoming visible. The results of other surveys suggest that the list of priorities is the same for candidates for employment of *any* age. These elderly people want to be part of the world of real work, and it is interesting to note that a commercial employment agency which supplies temporary elderly employees and gains its profit from the customary charges made on the employer can be a successful business concern.

It is curious that one of the major sources of the supply of elderly applicants to the commercial employment agencies are local offices of the Department of Employment – the so-called Job Centres. The range of ages covered by the Department, limited not by need but by statute, excludes at one end the young folk, anxious to end their period of pupillage, to start work and earn money but who must stay at school instead and, at the other end, the women of sixty and the men of sixty-five who are equally anxious to work but, so the community has decided, must for their own good go away and retire.

The situation now is that for the men and women at the bottom of the social pile, who have spent their lives as part of the organized multitudes in factories and who, for the most part, have filled their leisure time in pubs or at the lavish strip shows organized by the wealthy working-men's clubs, or, for the women, watching the coloured television or playing bingo – for these, retirement is the happiest state in which to pass later life. It has many compensations. Compared with the absolute necessity for labour, in default of which the grudging parish support once loomed so fearfully, the present status of the working-class elderly is enviable indeed. Nevertheless, in this present age of science and its elegant technology, freeing all of us, if we only learn how to grasp our freedom, to reflect on the purpose of life, there is surely scope to plan for something better.

Those who go in search of jobs when they are elderly are mostly from the middle classes who, during their younger years, have been accustomed to depend on their own efforts rather than on the diffuse corporate power, in many ways so like the power of nature, of their unions. The vacancies into which commercial employment exchanges fit these elderly applicants come, too, from what is, as yet, a minority segment of the community. It is interesting to speculate whether this minority will show itself to be the core of something which will grow bigger or, if it does not grow in numbers, whether it will develop in influence. Except for a constant demand for packers, or, as has been the case until recently, for temporary Christmas sorters for the Post Office, the main avenue for the employment of the elderly has been through small individualistic enterprises. The small head-office organizations of minor professional bodies offer good scope for elderly employees. If they had themselves belonged to the organization in question in earlier life, so much the better. Solicitors' offices provide opportunities for elderly workers, not only as clerks, but also as messengers and general factotums.

Although the manufacture and publication of books may be carried out as a trade on a large scale by a branch of a highly-capitalized, technically organized commercial enterprise – indeed, the proposition that best-selling paperback novels can not only be printed, packed and distributed but also written by computers is not altogether wide of the mark – one of the most remarkable phenomena in the world of ideas in Great Britain has been the survival, and often the proliferation, of small or medium-sized publishers. These, too, offer opportunities for the employment of elderly men and women. Charities, trade associations, chartered accountants, these and other organizations like them where groups of comparatively few are trying to achieve results on a comparatively individualistic scale, all provide opportunity for work by elderly people also trying to strike out for themselves.

Before leaving this somewhat specialized area of employment which, while not necessarily being of high intellectual or spiritual intensity, is perhaps the general mean of industrial and commercial work, it is worth noting another example of the provision of real work for elderly people. Marks and Spencer, as representing advanced and efficient thinking in retail trade, have, from the beginning, been intensely interested in the life which their employees enjoy, as distinct from the efficiency with which they contribute to retail trading. In conformity with the current social practice of the community, this firm normally makes provision for the retirement of men at sixty-five and for women at sixty. If, however, the people concerned would themselves *like* to continue working, they are free to do so provided they can show, when submitting themselves to an annual medical examination, that they are fit enough.

The narrative so far delineated in this chapter has traced the path from (a) the conception of the elderly state as being one in which work interpreted as a contribution to the economic activity of the community stops completely, through (b) a preliminary stage of organized hobbies and activities of sufficient complexity as to represent a stage almost mid-way between work and leisure, to (c) the ingenious organizations of the Link scheme, edging towards work but, while possessing much of the attributes of economic activity, carried out within a protected environment and operated as an activity restricted in the main to the elderly group themselves. Finally, there are those of the elderly who are prepared, regardless of the general current of thinking which, by and large, feels that they should be retired, to struggle on and continue to play their part as workers within the community.

Science can give no answer to the question: which is better, a life of bingo, bus outings with the Rotary Club and carpet slippers in front of the 'tele', or days as a filing clerk in a solicitor's office or as a 'floor spotter' – an occupation for the elderly which lends so much more dignity to the performer than if it were called a 'sweeper' – in Marks and Spencer? In fact, the question is not couched in appropriate terms. For those of a special bent, retirement can be the opening of a door to the good life. There are individuals to be found capable of living a full, happy life as a good companion, a staunch neighbour, a willing and efficient committee organizer, a helpful grandmother – or a gifted painter. Or, if we raise our eyes a moment from the pragmatic and utilitarian, albeit moral, world which even those we most admire have come to accept as the best we can aspire to, we can see that there have been other goals in different ages. For example, there was, two hundred years ago at the end of the eighteenth century, an ideal which commanded the adherence of the majority of educated people in Great Britain. This, when it succeeded, combined good sense, good manners and cultivated intelligence, rational piety and a spirited sense of fun. All these attributes, it could be argued, are attainable by the elderly as by the young, without any major change in the social structure, but merely a change in outlook.

Most people in the community expect to retire when current convention assumes that they should do so and, having retired, often find their life impoverished rather than enriched by the leisure which they find less satisfying than they had perhaps anticipated. Indeed, many people do not anticipate a satisfying period of leisure but are apprehensive about it before it comes to them. Others do what they can to avoid the leisure of retirement and try, at least for a while, to extend their years of work. There is, however, a yet smaller group of people, leaders of the community by virtue of their vigour and enterprise, who continue in active and creative life regardless of age. These, it can be said, take advantage of the extra period of active health and vigour which biological science, with its understanding of health and disease, is now able to provide.

Artists of all sorts, painters, musicians, sculptors, writers, actors, whose success at any age is due to their individual creativity, and who earn their living, so far as they are able to do so at any age, outside the conventional main stream of employment, continue to do so as long as their genius lasts. Those scientists who are in truth concerned with the understanding of the workings of nature, whether as manifest in chemistry (the science of the composition of matter), biology (which covers the processes of the living organism) or physics (which covers the understanding of energy and phenomena related to such understanding), are often found to be involved with their science to the day of their death. There is perhaps a particular significance in the fact that this is so. Many of those who can be described as scientists in the modern idiom spend their lives as members of what it is fashionable to describe as 'teams' and thus work as cogs in a complex and very expensive mechanism which can only be sustained by a heavily capitalized industry or by a state organization. The training of a haematologist who comes to work in the Regional Health Laboratory of a major local authority may be somewhat longer and more academic than that of the driver of an underground train operated by London Transport, nevertheless the character of the devotion demanded of the two workers, the haematologist and the driver, during the course of their day's work and the degree of responsibility with which the community expects them to act in dealing with a sudden emergency is not altogether different. When they reach retirement age, neither is likely to have been so deeply involved in the problems which have dominated the years of his working life that they will continue to occupy his thoughts during the years of retirement. For most people, fulfilment as a team worker can only continue during their membership of the team. But for the special kind of scientist – the real scientist – as for artists and writers, among others, the balance between what they do and are as themselves, and what they do as members of a group, firm or union (when they are doing what they are told) is more strongly weighted towards their personal than their social identity.

For those who as people are very much larger than the rest of us the idea of retirement can be seen hardly to apply at all as a milestone in the progression of life. Henry Moore, the sculptor, is a good example of an individual whose physiological efficiency is well maintained at a stage which, in conventional terms, would be described as old age. But it is not because he is in a fit state to supervise the construction of monumental pieces of stone sculpture in his ninth decade that he has a bearing on the present discussion. What is of greater significance is that no one would draw attention to the fact that he 'retired' from work (as a teacher in the Chelsea Art School with a monthly salary cheque and regular hours of work) more than a generation ago. Charles Dickens, although a poor example as a survivor, since he wore himself out and died in his sixtieth year, can nevertheless serve as another example of someone whose personal preoccupations – his drive to create by his writings – ranked higher in his scale of values than his 'employment' as what might today be described as a lobby correspondent in the House of Commons, from which 'employment' he retired – but not to a half-life of hobbies – at the age of twenty-five. The comparison is a valuable one: to take down parliamentary debates in shorthand and set them out ready to be printed in the newspapers is a form of writing in which an employee can find himself employed at a salary appropriate to the skill and training required to learn shorthand and to interpret in some kind of rational sequence the convoluted thought processes of the Members of Parliament. It is a job by which a journalist can expect to earn a living – and from which in due course he will be prepared to retire. On the other hand, to write *Pickwick Papers* is an act of creation by which the very core and heart of the writer is involved.

No one ever expected Sir Compton Mackenzie to retire. The word itself is inappropriate to the activities of a writer who, from his youth to his advanced old age, was so deeply involved with what he was doing that 'employment' for him was a word to describe what he was concerned with at that moment, not the designation, as defined within an appropriate job specification, of the class of work for which he had been engaged at a particular salary level.

The creative people whose attainments make them memorable do not become involved in employment. Nor do they retire. What is valuable to them, as it is also valuable to the community which recognizes their creativity, is their talent. Should this fail them in later life, it may not be callous for the rest of us to feel less regret at the decline in their economic status than at their more important impoverishment. The problems of retirement do not apply to men like Victor Hugo and Tolstoy. Both, driven on by their talents, played a significant part in the public life of their age. Hugo, a child during the turmoil of the Napoleonic times, glittered as an infant prodigy before his twenties from the fame of his poetry and went on to become a popular hero rewarded by Louis XVIII before he was twenty-five. By the time he was forty, he had made a new name for himself – not an altogether savoury one in the eyes of respectable people – by an outpouring of poetry in the new romantic vein. Another twenty years or so saw the violence of his politics leading to his flight and exile, later followed by a return to politics when his ideas came back into fashion. Throughout, it was his creativity that was his motive force and to the end of his life at eighty-three he continued to write. He died accepted, after all his ups and downs, as one of the greatest of his country's poets.

Tolstoy, too, wrote much as a young man. He completed *War and Peace* by the time he was thirty-six and his other great book, *Anna Karenina* by the age of forty-nine. Like Hugo, he was affected by the political and social climate of his times so that in his fifties he found his spirit moving him virtually to invent a new religion. He continued writing and preaching almost to the day of his death; indeed, some of his most poignant work was produced at the very end of his life when he was in his eighties. The idea of his being employed as the head of an agricultural commune – which, indeed, he was – from which he would retire on a pension at some predetermined retirement age is clearly ridiculous.

Can geniuses of such stature point to an appropriate goal for more ordinary people like ourselves? Examples of the great and distinguished come readily to mind. Bertrand Russell, whose reputation was first based on his academic attainments in mathematics and philosophy, continued into his eighties proclaiming his opposition to war: leading protests, and sitting down on stone pavements among radical protestors young enough to be his grandchildren. Verdi, Italy's greatest nineteenth-century composer, completed *Otello* at the age of seventy-three and then continued working at a great choral composition, *Stabat Mater*, which he completed when he was eighty-four, three years before his death at eighty-seven.

Today, such people are still to be found – Sir Adrian Boult is one – straddling the centuries.

Science is one of the great intellectual pursuits of the times. Most scientists at the start of their careers need to find employment like anyone else, in a university, a research institute, or an industrial research laboratory, at a salary which today is negotiated by a trades union, an association of university teachers, or a co-operative of medical consultants. Yet here again, for those more deeply involved (as are the real musicians regardless of the musicians union), with the secrets of nature, retirement and its problems can be irrevelancies. For Sir Rudolph Peters, sometime professor of biochemistry at Oxford, who discovered the function of vitamin B_1 in the life process, retirement, although it might have relieved him of the responsibility of talking at set times to large numbers of students, did not stop him thinking about the puzzles of biochemistry and continuing, into his eighties, to illuminate understanding of the intricacies of the chemistry of life.

Undoubtedly, there is need for those concerned with social administration to organize things so that the last twenty years of life, from sixty to eighty, are profitably used. Pensions, housing, medical attention and transport all need to be appropriately planned. But the problems involved must not be approached in isolation. The superstructure having been looked after, the fundamental challenge is to modify the activities of the technological society which we have developed – with all the many great benefits it brings – so that each citizen, at his or her level of capacity, can exercise the spring of creativity which all possess in a lesser or greater degree. The making of scientific discoveries, like painting masterpieces and writing books, involves long periods of hard and tedious effort. It is the spring of what I am calling creativity that drives the artist and the scientist to soldier happily on through all the difficulties of their work. The same applies to people like ourselves, who are more ordinary and have more ordinary ambitions. Consider the Post Office.

The postman who delivers the letters finds himself not merely serving as the last link in a distribution chain but playing an important social role as well. There are people for whom the postman's call is the emotional high spot of the day. For those people who live alone – and, as time goes by, more and more people do – the postman may be the only representative of the outside world who ever calls at the house, particularly if the milkman delivers while they are still in bed or, if they collect milk themselves with their other groceries, not at all. And the postman knows this. In country districts, he may be the driver of the only remaining form of public transport, and a personal friend of half the people he meets on the road. It is also interesting to note that as science is applied in more and more sophisticated forms and mechanical sorting is controlled by the phosphorescent bars on the first- and second-class stamps and by means of the phosphorescent dots of the postal coding system, the role of the human postman is in no way diminished. Though it is true that one human sorter aided by the coding mechanism can do a job which previously required seven sorters, the men and women thus released are required to deliver the post to the more numerous dwellings of a better housed and less overcrowded population.

Today, regular postal workers, like almost everybody else, retire at a set retirement age. Part-time and temporary postal workers go on as long as they are able – some of them to an advanced old age. They too, like the farm workers and the owners of old-fashioned corner shops which, though diminished in numbers, pertinaciously refuse to disappear, can enjoy what could also be called creativity through the infinite variety of services they render to the other members of the community. Postmen, however, represent a particularly interesting example because their role in today's society is integrated with the advanced technology of the times.

6 Measured in Money

On 4 February 1782, Parson James Woodford, the vicar of Weston a few miles from Norwich, entered the following item in his diary: 'To a poor old Man that plays on the Dulcimer gave 0.0.6.' A year later, on 5 February 1783, he noted: To a poor old Man with a Dulcimer gave 0.0.6.' And about Christmas each year he made an entry, similar to that for 25 December 1782: 'The following poor Old Men dined at my House to day, as usual. Js. Smith, Clerk, Richd Bates, Richd Buck; Thos. Carr – to each besides gave 0.1.0. – in all 0.7.0. I gave them for Dinner a Surloin of Beef rosted and plenty of Plum-Pudding. We had mince Pies for the first time to day .' The item entered for 11 October 1784 is: Gave poor old Mary Dicker this Morn' 0.1.0. She came to pay Rent for her House belonging to the poor Widows of this Parish.' These were benevolent contributions from the kindly parson, comparatively well off on his income of about £300 a year. His journal also has regular entries referring to payment of the annual poor rates based on the value of his land at 10d or 11d in the pound and coming to a half-year's charge of £1.5.2½ or, on another occasion, £1.12.2¼, or – this was 1787 – when the rate was 9d, reaching the sum of £1.2.8½. His entry on 27 September 1783 gives some idea of how the parish spent the money: 'went to see the Poor House on Sparham Hill, and walked over the whole House and saw the People in it. They all appeared comfortable – and the House cleanly kept both above and below – Forster walked over the

House with me. As I came away gave the Poor in it 0.1.0.'

At the time Parson Woodford lived, the population of England and Wales was about 7,800,000, of whom about two-thirds lived in the country and roughly one-third (2,500,000 in all) lived in the towns, though the industrial revolution had hardly begun. Although circumstances were so different then, the physiological phenomena of aging, for those who lived long enough to become old, were much the same as they are now. The social problems of our times are different, however. Firstly, we have exchanged personal and parish organization for the stratified communal structure which I have already described and, secondly, on the territory where Parson Woodford rode his horse, there are now 7,960,000 people of sixty-five years old or older, a number larger than the entire population as it was then.

The British community today, like that of other advanced technological societies, does know, in spite of what its politicians say, that industrial work of itself is not the fundamental purpose of life. People do recognize that the wealth our scientific and technological virtuosity provides makes it possible to do a whole lot of things which are more pleasant than work. Where there is need for discussion, thought and considerable intellectual ingenuity is in the development of a political and social mechanism by which, within the ambit of what is possible, we may find means to finance the diverse social aims we wish to achieve. Many people have given thought to how best to find the money for the proper support of the elderly. Until 1908 people were expected to do the best they could to take care of their own old age. If they were unable to support themselves there was little option but to go to the poor house and rely on the sort of additional provision Parson Woodford had described a century earlier. It was soon apparent that in an industrial age, a civilized and humane community had to do more. The decision was taken, therefore, to organize nationally a system which would provide for all those who could not help themselves a pension, amounting to about a third of the average working man's wage. This amount would be granted to a man for the support of himself and his wife if he could provide proof of his poverty. By 1925, a scheme had been worked out for collecting contributions during a man's working life so that a pension could be paid to him when he was old, whether he could prove his poverty or not. Then in 1948, after World War II, when, if ever, the community had a chance to assess the kind of future it was aiming for came the Beveridge Report. As a result of this every citizen was given the right to a pension when he was old, in recompense for the weekly payments he contracted to make throughout his working life.

The pension for a married man was, however, something less than half the average worker's income after tax and insurance payments had been deducted. In order to enable a pensioner with no resources of his own to live, a system of supplementary benefits was set up by which pensioners were entitled to claim if they were poor enough. No one believes that this system is entirely satisfactory, particularly when it appears that about 35 per cent of those who are entitled to the supplement fail, for one reason or another, to apply for it. But the scale of operations is formidable nevertheless. The magnitude of the charges are apparent when it is appreciated that the total income of the nation, as measured by the 'gross national product' is about £74,000 million, and that the amount paid out as pensions is nearly £400 million. These are mid-1970 figures.*

This is not all. Between 1936 and 1953, the number of working people who, with their employers, had organ-

* *Pensions – Where Next?*, M. P. Fogarty, Centre for Studies in Social Policy, London, 1975.

ized their own pension schemes doubled. By 1971, half the number of those in employment were involved in a pension attached to their employment, quite apart from their State pension. By the end of the 1970s the total payments coming from this source will be of the order of £4,000 million a year. Who is to say whether finding a total sum of nearly £10,000 million to pay out as pensions, representing little less than one-seventh of the gross national product is enough, too much or too little? The social arithmetic defies logic; it is like trying to make a value judgment between an orange and an umbrella. But the balance has to be struck, and the nation must decide how much of what there is to be shared should be allocated to education, to roads and railways, to the building of atomic power stations, to running the army, to the National Health Services, to opera, to lunar exploration (or, in the British case, supersonic air liners), and how much should be used to ensure a comfortable life for the elderly. But wherever the equilibrium is established, the sum of money needed to pension the elderly is a large one and the technical problems involved in making such finance available are intricate.

Even in communities where economic equality is accepted in principle, inequalities – between skilled and unskilled, lower-paid and higher-paid workers – do exist; no extra injustice is inflicted, therefore, and pre-retirement standards of living stand some hope of being maintained, if retirement pensions are also – to use the jargon – 'earnings related'. It thus happened that in 1975, a new British national plan was drawn up comprising six parts. The first provision was that everyone shall receive a basic pension; the second, that everyone who beforehand was better-off than most shall get, in addition, a supplement based on the degree to which his or her earnings during the best twenty years of working life exceeded the national average. The idea is that this addition, together with the basic allowance, shall bring a married couple's income up to something between 45 and 55 per cent of the average of those best twenty years. People who do not have twenty fat years among the lean will get proportionally less than those who do. The third idea in the plan was that those who through illness or accident find themselves incapable of going on working until the set retirement age shall receive a pension just the same. The exact amount, however, will depend on the age at which they gave up work.

The fourth point in the 1975 plan was the eminently sensible suggestion by which the supplement relating to a pensioner's previous higher-than-average earnings shall not be affected by the fact that he or she changed jobs and so obtained these earning from more than one employer. The fifth point aimed at establishing equality between men and women. Women marrying after 1978 will get pensions just like men. Housework will count as employment (thus restoring the word to its proper meaning). Naturally, since women are to receive the same benefit as men, they must pay the same national insurance too. One injustice only is to be retained: women are to retire at sixty compared with sixty-five for men. On whom the injustice falls depends on whether 'employment' is taken to be a blessing or a curse.

Finally, the 1975 plan allows employers to set up their own earnings-related pension schemes as an alternative to payment by employees of that part of the national insurance contribution which would provide the earnings-related supplement to the State pension. Employers can only contract out thus if they have made alternative provisions which are as good as, or better than, what the State would have provided. There are a number of complications attaching to this operation, covering such matters as putative pensioners and their employers changing their minds and wanting to rejoin the State scheme, and the need for employers to continually revalue what they do in order to keep it in line with the changing average of earnings.

Clearly, as time has gone by – from pre-Beveridge to Beveridge, and from pre-1975 to post-1975, great efforts have been made to improve the economic status of elderly people in Great Britain, as elsewhere. And other possible measures are being discussed. The most serious injustice, and one which sticks with greatest discomfort in the throats of well-meaning but actuarially-minded administrators, is the state of those who retired early ten, twenty, even thirty years before the more generous provisions were organized. These people, who after having devoted a sufficient period of time to work decided to start enjoying a different kind of life, all too often find themselves distressed in their old age. Their pensions, whether adequate or not when they were first paid, become less so as the average wage moves upwards year by year. And there are others who had no opportunity to clock up the necessary twenty years upon which calculations for earnings-related supplements depend.

Elderly people, like the annual rings within the growing substance of the trunk of a tree, are living history. Those who are seventy years old in the 1970s still see the world through the impressionable eyes they possessed in the 1910s when they were young and the idea of ever reaching the wealth and security of an affluence of £1,000 a year was a glittering ambition unlikely to be fulfilled. On the other hand the dread of parish relief and the poor house was very real. Intellectually, they know that the 1970s are a different era providing changed and radically improved conditions of life, but early impressions bite deep.

The overlap between people born at different ages – some in Queen Victoria's reign, some in that of Edward VII (myself, for one), others again for whom World War II is an historical event as hazy as the wars of Napoleon – is made more confusing by the simultaneous conjunction of elderly people of the same age yet with very different means of support. At the top are those enjoying what everyone can hope to achieve once the fiscal

machinery has been developed to make it possible. Here
are to be found retired senior civil servants and others
who once worked in the public service, together with
members of a few well organized business groups whose
pension schemes are so good that they possess a built-in
mechanism to make them proof against inflation. Such
schemes are only possible for those fortunate few capable
of drawing on some substantial source of funding or on
fiscal skills of exceptional virtuosity. This group, however, is rapidly being reinforced by all those who had the
good sense to be not too old to fit into the improvements
of the 1975 national proposals.

Side by side with these comes a second group for
whom things have not gone quite so well. Here are to be
found people receiving the basic national pension
together with what they had for the whole of their working lives thought of as an adequate and satisfactory
industrial pension. Quite often, however, their expectations are disappointed. Many of the earlier schemes
merely provided for a fixed annual pension, that is to say,
one fixed years before when the scheme was initiated, or
for a pension rising by, say, five pounds for each year of
the recipient's working life. Sometimes people, in the
pride of their youth, had terminated their industrial pensions, or had changed jobs in middle life and thus les-
sened their value. Pension schemes have in the past been
thought of – by both employers and employees – as a
reward for long and faithful service. But even with the
carefully-planned arrangements for industrial executives,
the final results have been disappointing. Calculations
made by the Institute of Management in 1976 showed
that a senior manager who changed his employer at
thirty-five, forty-five and again at fifty-five – surely an
estimable and not altogether uncommon thing to do –
could expect thereby to end up with 30 per cent less pension than a colleague earning much the same salary who
had stayed still for the whole of his career. Nobody wants

this kind of thing to happen. It is merely an illustration of the complexity of the mechanism which is needed to organize a pension scheme.

How many people in the middle of their working life has one not met grumbling about their jobs, about the company, the organization, or the service of which they are a part. How often has the conversation not ended with the remark: 'If it were not for my pension, I would chuck the whole thing up and leave tomorrow.' If they only realized that when inflation has had its way on the one hand, and the general standard of living has improved on the other, the pension so laboriously earned will be a disappointment when, on that memorable sixty-fifth birthday, it actually falls due. Perhaps it would be as well for the grumbler to take the plunge and quit the disagreeable job regardless of those distant consequences.

The third category of the elderly are those dependent on the basic pension, topped up, for those showing themselves to be lacking in alternative means, by supplementary benefits. This group comprises about one-third of pensioner households. Here are to be found people who retired long before occupational pensions and earnings-linked schemes began. In this group a smaller than average number own their own homes.

A special difficulty for those designing a scheme by which funds accumulated during the working life of a man or woman will provide support, in the form of pension, when he or she is elderly, arises from inflation. The active worker, in a time of inflation, can hope to balance the extra number of pound notes he has to pay for what he buys by the additional pound notes he receives at the end of each week or month. But what is the manager of even such a well-organized pension scheme as the Federated Superannuation Scheme for Universities – the so-called FSSU – to do when after putting by a lump sum for investment proportional to the earnings of each insured person at each stage of his or her career, he finds that the total sum is worth, in real terms, barely more than 20 per cent of the amount due under the original terms of the policy? So far as the traditional idea that pensions are a form of organized saving – whereby an individual, or a community, makes provision for old age by accumulating deferred earnings – is concerned, inflation makes it necessary to think of something else. Nor has it proved possible for the skilful manager of a pension fund – or, for that matter, for the State itself – to select appropriate industrial investments to counterbalance the effect of inflation, as made apparent by the fall in the value of the currency, when the most universally accepted procedure for holding back inflation is to impose an embargo on industrial companies paying out increased rates of dividends. Since pension funds are for the most part invested in industrial shares, if the normal value of the income from such shares is prevented from rising, the real value of the return from which the pensions are to be paid must inevitably fall.

A curiosity of the times is the action taken by the National Union of Railwaymen. Here we have an ancient union, based on the altruistic principles of socialism, whereby working men by combining can acquire strength to resist the harsh conditions which (history has shown) may be imposed on them by those whose interest is predominantly involved in the profits of the share-holders. Part of the weekly contribution of the union members is put aside to provide pensions for the contributors when they stop work in their old age. Those responsible for the management of the NUR pension fund, quick to assess the problems posed by inflation, took note of the fact that the value of paper money falls in relation to that of those permanent material objects to which people attribute real value. When inflation breaks all bounds and paper money loses its value altogether,

those whose economic status is still preserved are far-
mers possessing stores of food in excess of their own
needs. People with cellars full of coal are in the same
situation when the weather is cold. The phenomenon
was seen at the collapse of the Czarist regime in the Bol-
shevik revolution of 1917, and in the Weimar Rupublic
in Germany a little later, when the only currency with
which exchange could be achieved was durable, prefer-
ably portable property to which value was still attached.
In both Germany and Russia, silver teaspoons and gold
watches could be exchanged for food and fuel long after
roubles and marks had lost all value. It may be bizarre to
record that some millions of pounds of the NUR pension
fund was, in the far less inflationary early 1970s invested
in paintings, sculpture and objects of *vertu*, selected with
knowledge and judgment. Nor, as I write, has it been
shown that these articles will prove to be in practice sufficiently negotiable to provide the pensions which retired
railwaymen will expect to receive. Nevertheless, no one
who reads of the prices being obtained in salesrooms for
articles of quality would be prepared to assert that for
each million pounds expended on paintings and sculpture in the 1970s, much more may not be realized in, say,
the 2000s, when the time for paying out pensions to the
guards, porters and engine drivers of today arrives.

There are two questions to be answered. The first is:
are we agreed that a well-organized community should
provide an income for all its elderly members? Naturally,
everyone, whether young or old, would like to enjoy a
private income so as to be able – if this is what he or she
chooses to do – to live a life of idleness. Most people
would agree nowadays that such an income should be
provided for those who are sick and infirm. The notion
that once held currency that each individual, either alone
or as a member of a family, should take thought for the
future has gradually been abandoned, partly for technical
reasons (it is not possible to save in times of inflation)

and partly for moral reasons (it is thought now to be wrong and unjust for sons to inherit the estates which fathers have accumulated for their future). How large a subvention should be provided for the elderly is a much more subtle problem. Can the elderly do anything for themselves? They can, as most people who have considered the matter now agree, provide through the industrial pension schemes a proportion of their own income-linked pension. But can they not also through their own activities when elderly earn a part of their income, to the benefit both of themselves and of the community? The problem of pensions for the elderly cannot be considered in isolation, as I have pointed out before. There are other candidates for the community's largess. Whereas in some fortunate places – Saudi Arabia, perhaps, or Monte Carlo – it might be possible, if the community possessed the will to do so, to provide an ample subvention for every citizen throughout the whole of his life, in most communities, even in those enjoying a state of advanced technological development, the proportion of the communal income considered to be available for public welfare is limited. Generosity to the elderly must be balanced – and the elderly, in making a case for themselves must bear this in mind if they expect to justify their reputation for wisdom – by a recognition of the needs of children, of students, of the sick, as well as of those whose economic situation is the worst of all, namely parents with a low income and numerous children, and single-parent families.

Having reached the conclusion about what it is desirable to do to provide pensions for the elderly, the next problem is to find a way to do it. To start with, there is the cost of bringing into an improved national scheme all those older people whose pension level, when they first received their pensions, was lower than that provided for the younger pensioner who succeeded them, and who were lacking in the income supplement which the 1975 plan now proposes to provide for all. This cost, if it were to be met, would involve a single effort which would diminish as the less-well-provided elderly gradually died off. The major challenge is to implement the improvements in the general pension arrangements which everyone has agreed to be desirable. The contributions made jointly by employees and employers to pay for pensions amounted to 14 per cent of the income earned in 1975; according to the British Government Actuary, the amount will rise first to 16½ per cent and then steadily increase as the year 2020 approaches – and pensions planners must look ahead thus far – to 20 per cent of earnings. The magnitude of the technical problem involved in improving conditions for the elderly – as the 1975 plan proposed to do – can be judged by the size of the charge involved. The cost of raising the basic pension from one-third of the average earnings of the working community to one-half was calculated to be, in 1975 money, £2,500 million. And if people depending on unemployment benefit, sickness and widows' benefits and maternity allowances, all of which include a flat-rate fraction, considered that in equity they should receive the same improvement in their incomes as the elderly, the annual demand on the community would rise to the still larger sum of £4,800 million.

The technical problems involved in finding such gigantic sums continue to puzzle those who are expert in fiscal manipulation. But besides the sheer mechanics of the problem there are philosophical matters of principle. For example, Beveridge, the man who laid the coping stone on the great humane structure of the British welfare society, set out as a matter of principle to detail a system whereby the pensions to be enjoyed by an elderly citizen should be the accumulation of wealth laid by as weekly contributions during that citizen's working life. This principle, firmly based on sound arithmetic, common sense and a deep belief in the moral virtues of frugality, foresight and self-denial, is deeply entrenched. Through every change in government, pension contributions made by an individual to ameliorate his own old age, have always been free from taxation. Recently, however, a Select Committee of the House of Commons, seeking a way towards a more just society, explored the possibility of a 'wealth tax'. In the course of their deliberations they calculated that the capital value of each £1,000 a year's pension to which a member of an inflation-proofed occupational pension fund might be entitled possessed a capital value of £35,000. Faced with this piece of arithmetic, the members of the Committee, representing all shades of political opinion, failed to reach any conclusion as to whether the pension of, say, a senior civil servant should or should not be taxed as wealth (presumably to enable the State to be able to provide a pension for someone else).

If the Gordian knot were cut and the idea of frugal savings and personal contributions abandoned, the calculations would be easier. Citizens would receive their pensions because of their age and their citizenship. There would be no need for the individual to stick stamps on cards and for the Civil Services to employ people to count them. This would save some £250 million. But a greater saving still, as Professor Fogarty points out in his monograph, would be an acceptance of the philosophical view that the purpose of life is work rather than leisure, that science – aided by a reasonable modicum of luck – can stave off the disabilities and illnesses of age so that we would be justified, rather than reducing for ever the age of retirement, in postponing it from the present age of sixty-five until the age of seventy-five. This would virtually bring down the numbers to be provided for by two-thirds and reduce the annual cost to the British community from about £3,000 million to £1,000 million.

Such an eventuality is not at the moment an acceptable possibility. Nevertheless, a good deal of study has been given to the actuarial implications of providing pension schemes with some measure of flexibility. Even now there is provision for men and women who do not want to accept retirement at the due ages of sixty-five and sixty; they may leave their pensions undrawn for five years and receive an enhanced weekly amount when they reach seventy and sixty-five respectively. The actuaries have also calculated the implications of people being given some measure of freedom to draw their pensions earlier as well as later than the set age. Then there is the calculation of the effect of a uniform pension age for men and women, whether it be sixty or sixty-five.

Even though the notion of fixing a standard age for pensions at seventy-five, regardless of its economic significance (and perhaps, also, of its physiological impact: who knows what the effect of a good day's work might be on quite a number of fit old men and women), is not likely to be accepted as practical politics, the French pension scheme for the very old is worthy of note. This provides for a bonus of 20 per cent to be added to the national pension of former wage-earners after they have reached the age of eighty-five. It is clearly equitable and humane to provide more for people when they are very old and in need of what is inevitably expensive aid. But again, it is for the community a matter of balance. Was there, for example, a spare £450 million a year in Great Britain in 1975? If there had been, it could have been used to increase the pensions of those over seventy-five by 30 per cent. But perhaps the French were more subtle – as well as being more economical. To offer the bonus at eighty-five obviously costs less than to set it at seventy-five, at the same time it encourages all the eighty-four-year-olds to stick it out until their eighty-fifth birthdays. It is a common observation of those involved in geriatric medicine that their patients tend to defer their demises until *after* such notable events as their eightieth or ninetieth (sometimes even their hundredth) birthdays.

The complexity of the calculations to assess the cost of providing *more* for those who are very old and whose expenses are consequently greater needs to be balanced by thought about the implications of paying *less* to elderly people who, while they legitimately deserve a pension, can at the same time be expected to earn at least part of their own living. The Swedish Partial Pension Act of 1975 is an ingenious example of what can be done. To start with, it makes provision for workers between sixty and sixty-five who retire, to be sure, but only half way. If they work five hours a week less than they did before, but do work at least seventeen hours a week, they can draw a part-pension equivalent to two-thirds of what they are losing by not working full time. If on the other hand they do retire, they can earn as much as they are able on the side without diminishing their pensions by doing so. Furthermore, as in Great Britain, workers in Sweden can defer drawing their pensions from sixty-five until seventy and receive an enhanced payment when they do draw them.

A calculation which is as difficult to make in Sweden as it is in Great Britain or anywhere else is what the net effect of elderly people extending or restricting their working life will be. Obviously, if retirement occurs earlier, there will be an extra cost for pensions to be met. On the other hand, if some of those to receive their pensions were previously unemployed, there is a saving in unemployment payments by pensioning them. Delayed retirement, whether or not it involves some such arrangement as the Swedish part-pension scheme or the British earnings rule (which does not exist in Sweden), calls for the payment of an improved pension when the pensioner eventually takes it. There is also a further factor in the equation arising from the income tax payable by the more effective of the older workers whose earnings will attract the attention of the income-tax inspectors.

The elderly and their pensions illustrate in a particularly vivid way the delicate equilibrium that in every sort of society under every kind of government exists between what people do for themselves and what is done for them by others. In modern terms, those 'others' mean the State as a whole, once it implied something smaller: the family, the parish or, as in Scotland, the clan or tribe. In the United States, until very recently, people were expected to look after themselves out of their savings or their own insurance provisions. Failing such self-help, things were (and still are) hard. In communities such as exist in Great Britain and other European countries, there are, outside such savings as an individual can succeed in preserving in today's inflationary times, two main bases for the support of the elderly who cannot, or do not wish, to continue to work for money. The State pension schemes which we have been discussing form one base. The occupational pension funds operated by trades unions, by universities and by commercial firms form the other. As I have already commented, the managers of these funds – with the possible (and unproven) exception of those operating on behalf of the National Union of Railwaymen – have had to cope with the intractable problems of inflation quite apart from the inevitable guess-work of business judgment. Studies made in the mid-1970s by the British Institute of Management and the Centre for Studies of Social Policy found signs to suggest that companies and organizations which had been operating pension schemes, whether designed to cover everyone employed in the enterprise or merely those engaged in senior management capacities, were becoming discouraged. On the one hand, they were faced by the intractable actuarial conundrums, upon which I have already touched while, on the other hand, they saw that the improved State schemes for a combination of basic and earnings-linked pensions were, in fact, carrying out much of what they had proposed to do.

The managers of the State schemes, however, suffer from their own troubles. The sheer magnitude of the administrative problem of knowing the circumstances and entitlements of all those seven and a half million pensioners – if, indeed, it will only stay at seven and half million – so many of whom (and how irritating it can be) are restlessly moving about, losing their documents, trying to cheat, dying without notifying the pensions office and, in one way or another, turning themselves into those special cases which are such a trouble to a conscientious administrator. The proposal has therefore been promulgated* that two possibilities should be considered for the future, not one. As time goes by it may emerge that the mechanism of a State pension fund is not capable of the flexibility and responsiveness needed for the payment of occupational pensions to a diverse and increasingly enterprising community of pensioners, some younger, some older, some working, some working part-time, some leading a life of leisure, many with diverse histories of employment earlier in life. If this comes about, far from the State taking over the function of the sixty-five thousand existing independent pension funds of one sort or another (for such the number is), the occupational pensions movement, which, after all goes back two hundred years, with all its experience, diversity, skills, goodwill and popular esteem, might, in one of those unpredictable spins of the political wheel, be given the task of taking over the State's earnings-linked pensions operation instead.

On a more limited scale, the second idea is that there could be a choice between the use of either independent organizations or the State to supplement the pensions of

* *Pension Fund Socialism*, P. F. Drucker, The Public Interest 42, 1976.

the elderly. Here, too, we find entangled what individuals can be expected to do on their own behalf and what they can expect a well-run State to do for them.

There is ambivalence in the attitude of many advanced industrial communities to the question of whether a citizen should be encouraged to purchase his own dwelling or whether housing should, like water, policemen, education and medical treatment, be provided by the State. While social philosophy may argue in favour of the provision of communal housing, two factors support the opposite view. The first is a human urge to own the house one lives in, and the second is economics. The economic argument is a strong one. A man will dig his own garden, paint his own front door and paper the parlour without being paid to do any of these things. A public authority must employ a works department to execute these same functions. A tenant must pay rent all his life and accrue nothing for it at the end. An owner makes mortgage payments little different in magnitude from his neighbour's outgoings as rent. At the end of thirty or forty years however he possesses a substantial piece of real property which retains its value as a house regardless of the capricious fluctuations in the value of paper money.

This is an area about which choice between the community and the individual must be made. A second economic argument arises from the proposition that the real value of his house could be used to provide a significant proportion of an elderly owner's pension. In the United States, where self-reliance, on the one hand, and entrepreneurial alertness to fill any recognizable demand, on the other, have tended to be the main motives for action, a number of schemes are available to elderly people. The simplest is that they should mortgage their houses to underwrite an annuity. This implies that an insurance company accepts the actuarial bet of providing an elderly customer with a fixed income for the rest of his life, on the understanding that when he dies his house belongs to the company. More elaborate schemes involve an elderly couple, let us say, making over, not only their house, but all their investments and other property as well to a corporation which may have built an estate, complete with housing, a golf course, a gymnasium, games rooms, restaurant and, of course, swimming pool, where the inmates may be expected to spend the rest of their lives. Some of these schemes are excellently run, others are commercial enterprises which the contributors may find very much less satisfactory than they had been led to expect. An alternative middle course has been proposed in which, having bought his house from a public authority during his working life, a citizen can use it as security for a supplementary pension in his old age. On his death, the house then reverts to the community for the use of another generation. The organization of a technological society in which we can enjoy the fruits of science by which diseases are halted and long life assured for more people than ever before, in which air transport, food, clothing, television, warmth and comfort are available to all, is a difficult matter. Economics is one of the forces by which the political targets of society may be thwarted. Economics is not a science, yet its influence can decide whether science will be effective or not. A community may easily be strong, sophisticated and wealthy while at the same time sections of the population and, in particular, the elderly, are suffering from poverty. In this chapter, I have outlined some of the problems which have been overcome in order to provide the elderly with pensions, at a cost partly to themselves when young and partly to the goodwill of their juniors. In the main, the story is one of progress. The direction in which things have progressed, however, and in which they will progress in the future must be influenced by the goal at which the community is aiming. If people could choose, would they choose to retire earlier or later? Is it 'agism' to provide an old woman with a comfortable home or is it kindness?

Perhaps those who envisage a three-tiered pension plan may foreshadow the next move. This scheme envisages people choosing, first, early retirement, perhaps on a part-pension reinforced by an earned income, itself part of what was once a full wage. Next, as the young-elderly feel the desire for a more contemplative life, would come a period on full pension of which part might be the basic payment and part an earnings-linked or privately financed supplement. Finally, at some time between say, seventy-five and eighty, or at a point to be decided by the pensioner's state of health, a more generous pension would be paid to the old-elderly to meet the expenses inevitably incurred by the disabilities of advanced old age.

7 Better than a Walking-stick

It is encouraging to know that today the biological sciences can do much to prevent the diseases and disabilities of old age. Yet while much can be done to save those who might otherwise die of heart disease, and there has been some success in limiting the ills of certain cancers, and reducing the number of those attacked by senile dementia, still, not everyone can hope to escape ill-health. Even though in this age of scientific enlightenment the statistics of misfortune reflect the advantages that the current populations of industrial communities enjoy, each individual man or woman as he or she grows old is still – regardless of the assurances of scientific medicine – in the hands of God. One here and one there is picked out to suffer from arthritis, stroke or falling sickness. It is, therefore, encouraging to review something of what has been done by the application of reason, reinforced by science, motivated by good feeling (with which neither reason nor science have anything to do), to ameliorate disabled living among the elderly.

I separate reason and science by intent. Advanced science-based technology plays an important part in helping those who are singled out, it would seem, from their fellows, by the onset of disablement; but much can be achieved by simpler means. As was described in chapter 2, a human being's sense of balance and the co-ordination required for the seemingly simple yet mechanically complex process of walking erect on two feet deteriorates as time goes by. A simple yet effective means of improving the capacity of the elderly people for locomotion is to provide them with a walking stick. To furnish such a stick with a rubber tip may not appear to call for very much in the way of advanced technology, though the synthetic rubber from which the tip is made is indeed an intellectual triumph of little more than a generation ago, yet by such means the value of a stick for walking on the paved streets and plastic floors of a modern city is greatly increased.

Shall we describe it as science or reason to develop – as has quite recently been done – a stick which shall give added steadiness to an owner whose balance and ability to walk are more significantly impaired by fitting its lower half with three spread rubber-shoed legs?

A walking stick, whether it is of conventional design or modified to give firmer support must undoubtedly in its origins have been what Heinz Wolff would describe* as 'unexciting research into necessary equipment'. Wolff, at the Clinical Research Centre of Northwick Park Hospital on the outskirts of London, has been working to develop in different parts of Great Britain special units where efforts would be made to combine a variety of skills and produce all sorts of aids for the disabled, from the most technically sophisticated apparatus to the simplest gadget.

It is not easy to invent a really useful gadget. Everyone has come across devices which, however superficially attractive they may seem, turn out to be either ineffective or more trouble than they are worth. Let us, therefore – powerful intellectual thinkers all – not turn up our noses at a good gadget or strangle the research that may be needed to produce it. Few of those who are accustomed to eating a boiled egg set up in its shell in an egg-cup can appreciate the frustration felt by an elderly person

---

* *Practical Design for the Elderly*, H. Wolff, Old Age Today and Tomorrow, British Association, 1976.

with arthritis in one hand who, at breakfast, can do little more than knock the egg out of its egg-cup and chase it round the plate while unsuccessfully attempting to remove the shell. To overcome this problem someone needed to spend the time – and it has been done – to design a suck-on plastic egg-cup.

One of the paradoxes of history is the curious obtuseness of our predecessors in not making earlier what now seem to us to be very obvious discoveries. We are told by our teachers that so simple a device as a stirrup, enabling a rider to do things more efficiently on horseback without falling off, exerted a revolutionary influence on human history. Again, a fork seems nowadays so simple and useful a device, facilitating the eating of one's dinner in a clean and convenient fashion, that it is hard to remember that, in historical terms, it is a comparatively recent invention. Then there is the so-called 'sailing-ship syndrome': it was only *after* the sailing ship had become obsolete as a serious means of transport that the real improvement in its performance took place. This was the development of fore-and-aft sail arrangements, by means of which modern yachts would have outsailed the tea clippers which were thought, in their time, to be the ultimate in efficiency. My point is that only when people really put their minds to the solution of a practical problem does real progress occur. Many of the advances of the industrial revolution owed little to science and could have been invented at any time. The Romans, for example, could have made a bicycle if they had only thought about it. Much can be achieved without science and by quite simple means. For instance, there is no need for computer-controlled robots to be invented to help elderly people who have only got one good hand or one non-arthritic arm to feed themselves. A non-slip mat impregnated with sticky wax and a perfectly ordinary plate can give such an elderly person independence at meal-times. A clip-on rim to the plate together

with a special knife with a sharp curved blade can enable
an old person to cut up his or her meat with one hand by
merely rocking the knife, without needing a fork to hold
the roast beef steady. This kind of knife is in fact fitted
with tines so that it can be used as a fork as well as a
knife.

Life for the elderly can be made more agreeable and
effective by the application of science, as I shall describe,
but much can also be achieved by taking thought of
what needs to be done and by an active determination to
improve matters. It is not a matter of high science –
although science may come to be involved – to make it
easier for arthritic elderly people to dress and undress
themselves. Active people in the prime of life put on
their shoes and take them off again with so little mental
and physical effort that they overlook the fact that once
upon a time they had to learn how to do it and that, their
muscles and joints being in good working order, they
employ a considerable degree of physical flexibility in
doing so. Someone must, therefore, on behalf of the
infirm elderly, study the operation and make it easier to
perform. Who knows, apart from contributing to the
comfort and self-respect of the elderly, the successful
researcher into the putting on and taking off of clothes
may make a fortune. After all, Whitcomb L. Judson in
1891 was merely attempting to design a mechanized system for doing up the rows of hooks and eyes on the outside of ladies' calf-length boots when he stumbled on to
what became the zip-fastener and thereby, besides making himself a lot of money, brought to an end the long
supremacy of buttons and button-holes.

Gadgets, quite apart from the more sophisticated
equipment by which the disabled elderly can benefit, fall
into several categories. Besides those which make eating
and drinking, dressing and other such domestic operations, such as washing and taking a bath, and attending
to the wants of nature easier and less troublesome, there

is a second category relating to the architecture of the houses in which elderly people find themselves living. For example, if climbing stairs becomes a problem, it can be tackled either by devices which make the stairs easier to negotiate or by organizing life in a bungalow or a flat on one level. Much else can be done. Elderly women who throughout their lives have expressed themselves through their cooking, and have contributed, through the meals they have created, to the corporate life of their own family and to the wider social group around them, can continue with this commendable form of self-expression if their kitchens are intelligently designed to take account of the diminishing physical capabilities of their old age. Similarly, gardening – that domestic art in which so many British citizens excell – is something which appropriately modified tools and methods can enable the elderly to enjoy. The humanity and creativity – not to mention the possibility of nutritional, aesthetic and economic return – attaching to this most civilized activity is exemplified in the involvement of some of the greatest of the nation's gardening enterprises in the modification of techniques in order to meet the requirements of age and infirmity. Exhibitions of what is possible have been mounted at the Chelsea Flower Show since 1967. The Royal Horticultural Society has done the same. London, too, has taken a hand with a demonstration in Battersea Park. Virtue would indeed reap a reward if the 'zip-fastener effect' came into operation and out of all this there emerged a technique of applicability to both elderly and non-elderly gardeners.

Furniture can also be designed with the convenience of the elderly and the disabled in mind. To start with, chairs, tables and the like can be made to the proper height and constructed so that they do not tip up and topple over. This is just a beginning. Much more can be done in a common-sense way, as any normal person, whether old or young, who has struggled with a stuck drawer or a wardrobe door that will not stay shut can testify. The introduction of a modicum of science can make much more possible. The layman who has seen a young girl in a garage lift up a two-ton motor car on a hydraulic lift may – if he thinks about the matter at all – view the whole thing with amazement. The same sort of thing can be done using compressed air in place of the compressed hydraulic fluid. The principle of the hydraulic ram (when a fluid is used) or of the transmission of pneumatic force (when air or some other gas is employed) is an interesting one. The application of what may seem to be a comparatively small force to a narrow pipe can achieve a remarkable amount of work when the pressure is spread out over a wide area.

Consider the case of an elderly man, in full possession of his faculties, taking an interest in life and, in return, enjoying the respect of his family and friends. He is, however, very old and in consequence is less mobile than he once was. Nevertheless, he is quite capable of getting out of bed and can move unaided to his favourite chair. But when he comes to get up out of the chair, he finds it difficult to do so. No one may be about at the appropriate time. The consequence is that when in due course someone does notice his predicament and comes to his call he has wet his trousers. This can be far more than a trivial misadventure. His daughter-in-law, already fully committed to her children, her husband, and her domestic duties, can be forgiven for finding the extra laundry, the disagreeable work of cleaning up the mess and, above all, the failure such an incident represents to maintain the standards of seemliness and decorum which are so important for each one of us, more than she can tolerate.

The solution to the problem, the prevention of so much damage to the old man's self-respect and perhaps to the happiness of his remaining years, not to mention the distress at his seeming incontinence suffered by his children, his wife and his friends, may be a simple appli-

cation of the principles of pneumatic science. It is easy
to fit our elderly man's armchair with an inflatable plastic bag in the form of a seat cushion. This can be slowly
inflated by pressing a button which starts up a blower
similar to those found in ordinary domestic vacuum
cleaners. The bag is capable of producing a pressure of
about one pound per square inch, which is sufficient to
elevate anyone sitting on it into a standing position
without the need for chains, gears, springs or any other
apparatus capable of causing injury.

A pneumatic system of this sort can be used for a variety of things. The actual part that does the moving,
whether it is a seat cushion to raise the user from a sitting to a standing posture, or an apparatus intended to
turn over in bed someone suffering from an attack of
rheumatism, can be made cheaply from plastic. This
means that it can be made the shape and size suited to
the function it is required to perform. If it becomes dam-
aged or gets dirty, it is inexpensive enough to allow for it
being thrown away. The fan unit to generate the one-
pound-per-square-inch pressure can be interchangeable.

An entirely different system but one that is equally
simple and can be equally inexpensive is based on the
principle of a car jack. This also can be coupled to an
armchair so that an elderly person can pump himself or
herself from a sitting to an upright position. Both a jack
and a vacuum cleaner are familiar and understandable
implements. Heinz Wolff has pointed out that such
understandability can be important in two respects.
Firstly, even when a piece of equipment can be shown to
be useful to an elderly person coping with the disabilities
of age, it may, by its novelty, so puzzle and upset those
for whom it is intended that they do not take advantage
of the benefits it could offer. The telephone is today
widely recognized as a valuable social tool, facilitating
both the exchange of human good feeling and such
mundane operations as contacting the plumber; yet

there are still to be found individuals, born and brought up in the early decades of the century when the telephone was an incomprehensible and – for some – frightening piece of apparatus, who are nervous of using it. Some of the newer technological devices developed for the use of elderly infirm men and women can frighten them by their seeming complexity in the same way, or worse, the elderly may not even know of their existence. But even when a device is not of itself particularly complicated, its introduction may come up against the innate conservatism which is common to us all and which tends to become more pronounced as we grow older. After a lifetime of doing things in a certain way in her own kitchen, perhaps organizing meals for a family, an elderly woman, even though she may know in her heart that she is no longer capable of lifting heavy saucepans or stirring a stiff mixture in a mixing bowl, may feel a strong psychological resistance to doing things differently – even when the advantage of doing so is explained to her by a highly-qualified scientific expert.

This brings us to Heinz Wolff's second point of argument. When it is possible to make use of a scientific principle in a simple and non-mysterious way, it may be possible to involve a wider spectrum of the community in the operation than merely the putative beneficiaries. Those few elderly people who still feel distrustful of the telephone can be talked out of their unease more readily if the persuasion of their grandchildren is added to that of the representative of the welfare service by whom the telephone is being specially installed. Similarly, while the basic conception of – let us say – pneumatically-operated aid systems may be a product of a scientific research unit, the specific modification required to suit some particular individual circumstance may be designed in the currently well-equipped workshops of a comprehensive school or polytechnic. Where such an activity can be organized as an offshoot of a sensible and imaginative educational plan, the knowledge of what is afoot becomes widespread so that the elderly disabled and those in the local community simultaneously become more generally aware of what is being done and consequently of what is becoming available. When the time comes for the elderly to put these gadgets to practical use they have, to a major degree, been demystified.

The special equipment for the elderly and incapacitated, if it is to be effective, must be endowed with two sets of qualities. Firstly, it must be technically efficient. This is the aspect which brings into play the natural sciences, occupied with the diverse principles of engineering. Secondly, since the abilities and disabilities of no two individuals are identical, nor are their circumstances likely to be the same, apparatus must always be modified to suit the needs of its specific user. There is good reason to suggest, therefore, that the modification of equipment to suit individual requirements together, perhaps, with the actual construction and distribution of the equipment, is the kind of 'employment' which could be fitted into those lengthening periods of our lives when we are active but without pay: when we are retired, unemployed, studying or on holiday. Today's citizens are, in fact, on holiday for about twenty-three fifty-seconds, that is just over half, of what we call our 'working life'. This fraction is made up of, say, four weeks holiday, two weeks of Christmas and New Year, another week of miscellaneous bank holidays and fifteen weeks represented by the one hundred and four Saturdays and Sundays when no modern member of Christendom expects to work.

In Germany, there is an organization called, if one may freely translate its title, the Good Will Company, which does just this work. It is in some respects similar to the Link Organization scheme described earlier. It is made up of retired craftsmen of all sorts who specialize in modifying and installing equipment in the homes of elderly people. There are two aims. One is to help the very elderly people who need the devices and improvements. The other is to familiarize the members of the Good Will Company in the full vigour of their sixties with what they too will need to use and understand when they are in their eighties and nineties.

To look through the massive compilations gathered together in Great Britain under the title of 'Equipment for the Disabled' by the Oxford Regional Health Authority, brought up to date every year, and in Sweden by the ICTA Information Centre, situated in the town of Bromm, is to marvel at what so-called 'unexciting research into necessary equipment' can achieve when its results are sensibly applied. A simple bracket that fits over the knee of an elderly woman as she sits can provide at its upper end a convenient support for her sewing or embroidery, and enable her, despite stiffness in the joints of one hand, to be usefully and creatively employed instead of waiting for those long hours to pass. Or again, an even simpler device, a rod with a rubber tip, can constitute a 'dressing and undressing stick'. During our thoughtless period of maturity, we forget the furious frustration we suffered as children unable to get our arms into the right armholes of a shirt or dress. The elderly understand the physical contortions required for the successful completion of such activities. A properly designed stick can greatly facilitate dressing and undressing by meeting the exigencies of the geometry of a particular garment, on the one hand, and of the human frame, on the other. All that is needed is for someone to study this geometry and then work out the appropriate procedure to overcome its rigidities.

A subtler exercise in applied geometry is the 'plastic stocking aid'. This consists of a slice of smooth plastic, firm yet flexible, of a shape which enables it to be bent over the upper part of the ankle and shin. It thus constitutes a bridge along which a sock or stocking can be drawn. This device, a scientific development based on the principle of the shoe horn, facilitates to a remarkable degree a manoeuvre which elderly people often find troublesome.

There are plenty of dressing-aids available. 'Equipment for the Disabled' includes a complete supplementary report on 'Clothing and Dressing'. As with the problem of going up and down stairs, the solution to difficulties in robing and disrobing can take two forms. On the one hand, are devices by which operations that have become difficult can be made easier and, on the other hand, there are ways – as in moving to a bungalow where there are no stairs – of avoiding the troublesome manoeuvre altogether. Quick-change artists in the music halls have used these for years when the whole of an evening dress suit – white tie, stiff shirt, cutaway coat and even the dress trousers – does up all the way down the back. The problem for the elderly who are becoming infirm first needs to be recognized, then it needs to be thought about, and then the solution, sometimes complex and requiring advanced science and technology but sometimes soluble by simple means, may be worked out. Do not let the scientist or, for that matter, the medical expert consider beneath his dignity so simple a device as a knotted tie fitting snugly into an elderly man's collar, of which the part concealed under the man's shirt-collar is not the substance of the tie at all but a piece of elastic. The device can be made a mite more technological if, in place of old-fashioned elastic, there is attached to each side of the tie-knot a tab of 'Velcro'. This is a plastic material with minute plastic bristles. The bristles of the two tabs engage under the collar and hold the tie in place. Simple as such devices may seem, they relieve the wearer of at least part of his humiliating dependence on a harassed nurse or a supercilious granddaughter to whom he would otherwise have to turn to get his tie tied.

Domestic tasks are often tiring and slow to perform. There are two reasons why this is so: no one has studied them, and active, healthy people often enjoy what they are doing so that there is little reason for them to do things quicker and more efficiently. For the elderly, however, who may not have the strength to accomplish the work, there is a real need to study what is to be done and to find the best way of doing it. And who knows, when the necessary aids have been designed for the old and frail, they may appeal to the young and strong as well. For example, husbands purple in the face in their efforts to unscrew the stopper of a jar of home-bottled plums may welcome the simple tool, the 'Seiger Twist Jar-opener', or one of the other convenient kitchen vices by which a variety of food packs can be opened without any of the struggles in which ordinary citizens find themselves involved. Simple clamps; bread-buttering boards which hold the slice still while the butter is applied; knives, forks and spoons with handles designed (as normal cutlery is not) to fit the hands of those who use them; gas taps and electric switches more easily, safely and accurately controlled than those we members of the general public put up with – all these have already been designed to help elderly people live as full a domestic life as they choose while medical science searches for the means of preventing rheumatic and arthritic conditions and the physiological deterioration of old age. My favourite simple invention for the elderly is a clamp to perch on one's shoulder into which the telephone can be clipped so that one can converse with both hands free without having to learn the trick, by which so many non-Americans have been defeated, of squeezing the receiver between one's jaw and one's shoulder.

Not all the simple inventions are for the basic needs of the day, for dressing, cooking, sitting safely on the lavatory and getting up again. There are others to facilitate the lighter side of life. Elderly bridge-players who find difficulty in holding their cards need have no apprehensions of having to give up their favourite game. A hand of cards can conveniently be set out in order supported between the bristles of an inverted scrubbing brush. Much more fancy holders are available, but the scrubbing brush serves just as well. Reading or watching television while flat on one's back are possible too. So called 'recumbent spectacles', fitted with prismatic lenses and operating on the same principle as a periscope, allow both these luxuries to be enjoyed with ease. What, it can be asked, have we younger folk been missing all these years?

Simplicity, aided by thought, can, it seems, do much. Of course, much more can be done when some of our modern technological capabilities are brought into play. A pneumatic system to help an elderly person turn over in bed can be a useful aid indeed. There are people who have become stiff and immobile who also find the change from the vertical to the horizontal posture difficult to accomplish. For these there is a bed which they can approach when it is upended vertically and supported on its end-board. The putative sleeper stands on this board as it rests flat on the floor, and leans back against the upright bed. A touch of the switch puts the mechanism in motion and the whole thing gently moves itself through ninety degrees, ending up with the elderly person comfortably settled in a recumbent position.

Of a similar degree of mechanical complexity is the wheel-chair fitted with a battery-driven electric motor. With this, the disabled person can move easily about the house and garden. An ingenious device fitted to the front of the chair allows it to climb up on to the curb and climb down again. When the chair is out of use, its batteries can be plugged into the mains and recharged.

A further step forward in technological sophistication is represented by a piece of electrical control equipment, of which the 'Possum Environmental Control System' is a widely used example. This allows the elderly person to control his house from an armchair, as a captain controls his ship from the bridge. The apparatus is operated by a switch which can be activated by hands, feet, elbows or, indeed, by blowing or sucking, if this is more convenient. How long the switch is pressed the first time determines which of ten or so horizontal columns will be selected. The second press on the switch decides which of the items in the column selected has been chosen. There can be a column for answering the telephone, with one slot for starting the conversation and – as is essential even for less highly mechanized telephones – another slot for stopping it. Suppose the doorbell rings. From his chair, the old gentleman can switch on the intercom and find out who is there before he (or, of course, she, if the operator is an old lady) decides whether or not to activate the appropriate slot to open the door. There can be provision for several intercom systems in different parts of the house. Other columns are designed to turn on and off various lights, or to raise or lower the thermostat control of the central-heating system. Naturally, there is a column of alternatives for the television – to select a particular programme, to increase or decrease the volume. A similar system controls the radio and, for better equipped households, another position operates the record player and the tape recorder. Special provision is also made for a position on the machine to sound an alarm so that the elderly operator can summon assistance should the need arise.

Modern electronics provide many possibilities for ameliorating the life of infirm elderly people. If it should happen, perhaps after a stroke, that the old man or woman has difficulty in speaking, a device equipped with a rudimentary keyboard, something like a miniature typewriter, can be of help. In the simplest form of this instrument, messages tapped out on it appear on an unrolling strip of paper tape. In the more sophisticated version, the message appears on a screen, stays visible long enough to read and then fades away. There are a variety of such 'light-writers' now coming into use.

All this, however, is only a beginning. We have all had time to become acclimatized to life as it is now in the electronic age and know that much more is only just around the corner. One has already met the up-to-date housewife who, in the middle of a conversation, pauses while the alarm in her digital watch buzzes to remind her, either that her oven has turned itself off or that she should send some kind of pulse to the mechanism in her kitchen to set some cooking process in motion. Machines for washing clothes are a commonplace; they link together a chain of operations whereby without human interference, the washing process is followed by a series of rinsing stages which themselves, after the last of the water has drained away, lead on to a drying operation. While so far the machinery does not iron the articles it has washed, and put them away in a drawer, chemical advances have to quite a large degree done away with the ironing process altogether by the development of elegant drip-dry textiles made of petroleum. No longer, as described by Pepys in the seventeenth century, by Parson Woodford in the eighteenth century and by Dickens, with his mangles in the back kitchens of the nineteenth century, is wash-day a major domestic undertaking.

Dish-washing machines are also accepted as commonplace. We forget that in their memory systems are the instructions telling them to heat the water to an appropriate temperature and no hotter, to wash the crockery, rinse it and, after having dried it, to turn the mechanism off. One no longer sees a kitchen-full of people, working together, talking together and living together – with the washerwoman and the man washing the dishes often the oldest of the lot.

To today's technologist, the memory system of a washing machine or of a dish washer is elementary Model-Ţ stuff. A schoolboy's calculator can do more. We can, therefore, confidently predict that the various research establishments which are working to develop a completely automated and computerized memory system for the elderly will quite soon, and not necessarily at very great cost, come up with electronic apparatus capable of looking after elderly people as well as any human companion. Or, to put the matter the other way round, such apparatus will go a long way towards enabling elderly people to safely look after themselves.

In a hospital, a 'bleeper' carried in a doctor's pocket can do just one thing, that is, bleep when someone wants to attract his attention. The sort of radio set carried by a policeman on the beat can do two things – attract his attention and, having done so, allow him to get in touch with his headquarters. The possibilities of miniturization will allow very much more to be done. A microcomputer incorporated in a cash register can remember what transactions have taken place in the shop and can also protest if the wrong change is given, if there is insufficient stock available to fill an order, or if the wrong price is charged. Alternatively, it can, all by itself, make a telephone call to remedy a situation which is likely to lead the shopkeeper into difficulties. Similarly, it is entirely feasible to equip an elderly person with a device which, should he or she decide to make a cup of tea, will sound a reminder after the appropriate length of time has elapsed that the gas is still on and should be turned off. The same device could be designed in such a way that, should the person carrying it fall, it would send out a radio signal which would activate a telephone programmed to call a designated number and play a taped message explaining to the rescue services – whoever they are – what has happened and to whom.

There are almost no limits to what could be achieved. Programme an old lady whose memory is fading but who, in her prime, enjoyed as her greatest pleasure fame as a cook, and the electronic memory will, should she wish to enjoy the pleasure of reliving her old culinary dexterity, stop and remind her each time she forgets an ingredient or goes to add salt when the recipe calls for baking powder. Most useful of all, if she becomes confused while out shopping the device could tell any strangers trying to help her what her name is and where she lives. It could refuse to allow her to shut the front door until she could satisfy it that she had her latch key with her. It could tell her to turn off the taps if, when running a bath, she returned to the living room on an errand which took more time than she had anticipated. Of course, there would be no real difficulty in arranging for the mechanism to turn the water off itself.

It is interesting at this point to review the scene. Here, we have the Disabled Living Foundation, a distinguished organization based in London, with professional direction of the highest order, and trustees who, besides representing leaders of the community, number among their members medical and scientific experts at the forefront of their professions. Similar organizations exist in Sweden, in Canada and elsewhere. Within the collection of equipment gathered together by the Foundation are, at the one extreme, sophisticated examples of the most advanced computerized electronics – although the control and guidance system which I have just sketched out does not yet exist in all its luxurious proliferation – all the way to the simplicity of an armchair with a spring under the seat to help the sitter to get up, an inverted scrubbing brush or a walking stick.

Each of these pieces of equipment is valuable in its proper context. Ingenuity and thought have gone into its development and the life, freedom and independence of elderly people have been enhanced therby. The work which has been going on to publicize what has been done, what is available and what the advancing frontier of bioengineering will undoubtedly make available in the future is very valuable. Perhaps, however, there is a reason why the simpler solutions to some of the problems of disability – the ingenious slings for hoisting elderly bathers into and out of their baths, the rails and other devices for improving the convenience, comfort and safety of the lavatory, the strong yet light trolly to serve both as an aid to walking and as a means of transporting the teapot and the cups and saucers from the kitchen into the living room – have attracted more attention and may even have done more good than the more sophisticated (and very much more expensive) products of advanced technology.

Young children, like some very elderly peole, are incompetent. To remedy this incompetence we send them to school to learn. Nowadays, however, bioengineering of exactly the sort I have just outlined can be used to teach them. Arithmetic and algebra, Latin and French, spelling and physics – all these can be instilled by way of a properly programmed teaching machine. Such a machine will deal with imperturbable patience with the stupidest pupil. When the child makes a mistake, the teaching machine will correct it. Whereas it will slowly spell out a problem for a dull learner, it will move swiftly ahead for a bright one. It would appear that everything is to be said in its favour, that its memory, in which the knowledge it has to impart is stored, can be filled with the highest wisdom there is about the subject under instruction. Yet while all this is true, while there are circumstances in which a modern electronic teaching machine (or the old-fashioned paper-and-ink device which preceded it: I refer to a book) is the best instructor there is, there are other circumstances in which a human teacher is better. Children acquire more from their teachers than the facts given in a book about history or arithmetic. And they also get more from their days at school than from private communion with a teaching machine. This realization has a bearing on the elderly and their situation, too.

Bioengineering can do much to give disabled elderly people mobility and independence. The progression from the simple and not particularly effective ear trumpet which I can remember, from the time when I was a child, being pointed in my direction by my deaf aunt, first to the cumbersome electrical device set down on the table and coupled to the user's ear by a length of wire, to the modern miniature hearing aid is a record of steady and rapid advance. We can have justifiable pride in the scientific discoveries which have been made in the past thirty years or so – it is salutary to remember that Bardeen, Brattain and Shockley were awarded the Nobel Prize for developing the transistor, upon which almost all our modern electronics depend, as long ago as 1956.

The replacement of arthritic hip joints by quite large and complicated steel and plastic substitutes is being achieved by major advances in surgical and engineering techniques. This work is giving years of new life and happiness to those of the elderly who would otherwise be almost completely immobile. The ingenious gadgets and devices designed to help elderly people cope with everyday life can, too, bring comfort and happiness to those who need them.

Clearly, what we must do, then, is find a way to strike a balance between the use of simple devices, such as walking sticks and inverted scrubbing brushes, spoons with big graspable handles, and the marvels of advanced technology. Both have a place. The automatic telephone exchange which, besides connecting us with a distant number – for all we know, bouncing the message off an artificial satellite hanging suspended over the Atlantic Ocean – is a useful device for improving the quality of life for everyone, whether young or old. On the other hand, devices so subtle that they take the place of human companions may convert 'independence', which is today generally thought of as a good thing, into 'isolation', in just the same way that 'leisure' (a good thing) when extrapolated out of context can become 'unemployment', which is universally accepted as evil. The alarm system which an elderly person could carry about and which would telephone for help should its possessor fall, would be an excellent device warmly to be welcomed. On the other hand, the research unit in the university where it is invented would best justify its claim to universality if at the same time it could point to ways in which we could organize the community's social life so that old people did not too frequently find themselves alone. It may be impossible to find fault with a device that can be infallibly depended upon to prevent us from locking ourselves out of the house or pouring boiling water in the teapot without first putting in the tea, but it is equally impossible to love it.

Perhaps, however, this is not the business of research scientists in universities.

8 What Now?

As the twentieth century moves towards its close, new ideas are being generated in all sorts of directions. The student revolt – in France, in America, in Japan and in Great Britain – has come and gone. The status of women in Western society – and even, here and there, in Islamic societies – has been reassessed. Past notions about what is now called 'racism' have changed, as have views about women, involved with what is called 'sexism'. Now, even if so far restricted to the United States, another sin has been created, 'agism'. All of these new ideas have had some protagonists who have pushed their claims, derived from the new possibilities of the scientific age, beyond the limits of reason. Nevertheless, the achievements of science, in making practical things possible and in changing our ideas about the nature of the world in which we live, justify the new conceptions which are being worked out.

So far as aging is concerned, science allows us, firstly, to map out the physiological changes that occur as we gradually mature and move from one stage of life to the next. More significant than this, however, has been the influence of medical science on the number of us who can expect to survive the great killing diseases of the past – cholera, typhoid, the multifarious sicknesses of childhood, tuberculosis so recently tamed – allowing us to enjoy the old age which was not reached by so many of our predecessors, and the new knowledge which permits an increasing proportion of those of us who do survive to enjoy in good health the later decades of life. All this is important; it is also interesting to follow how it has come about. At the same time it is fruitless to pursue with delight and admiration the progress of those who are so skilfully elucidating the causes of dementia and stroke and putting right the disabilities of arthritis and incontinence if, at the same time, we give no thought to the place of the elderly, now endowed with health and vigour, within the society of which they are members.

The diversity of the activities in which today's elderly people take part is remarkable. There are those who pay little attention to the conventional status of retirement and continue with the activities they enjoyed before. These people are aware that the physiological changes which are part of aging occur at different ages in different individuals. A dramatic example of an elderly enthusiast was the man who had been an airman in his youth who took up gliding and continued with this hobby, together with long-distance fell walking, into his seventies. At the age of seventy he enrolled in a course as a parachute jumper and, being impelled by those in charge of the instruction to do so, underwent a physical examination which showed that he was fit to jump.

In the same category as this is the Walsall man in his eighties who keeps himself in practice as a gymnast on the trampoline! There are numerous examples of elderly people who join together in pursuit of some combined activity. In Halifax is to be found the Autumn Tints Old Comrades Cycling Club. The members are seventy years old or older. They meet about once a month for a cycle tour. Individual members, however, travel further afield and can be found across Europe, while two of the elderly cyclists achieved celebrity by cycling across the entire width of the United States.

Operating at a lower level of physical activity is one enterprising group of elderly people in London. London is a city which provides the elderly with a permit allow-

ing them, within certain hours, to travel without payment on the buses. The group organizes tours to remote
but interesting parts of the metropolis. Considerable
intellectual activity is involved in administering the
scheme, in identifying places to be visited, and in working out the combination of buses by which the goal is to
be reached. Nor is the physical effort needed for getting
on and off the buses and for suffering their vibration
while on them by any means negligible. A variant of this
communal touring is the elderly couple who started in a
sedentary fashion reading about the history of London in
their local public library and who then worked out ways
of visiting by bus what they had read about. A special
complication, with which they taught themselves to deal,
was the way to see the sights in which they were
interested and yet complete the outward and return journeys within the period during which their bus passes
were valid.

An orchestra in Sheffield is made up of elderly people
from all over the city. Many of them were amateur players when they were younger, although some of them
have learnt to play only since they retired. What they
lack in the higher musical skills, they more than make
up for in enthusiasm. Again, physical endurance is
required as well as aesthetic appreciation: there are complicated cross-country journeys to be made by the players
to get themselves to the church halls where the rehearsals are held; there are the rehearsals themselves; and,
finally, there is the tension of a public appearance, even
if it is only in a remote town hall.

All this is better than shuffle-board. And the fact that
it might still be stigmatized as 'play', could be taken to
reflect on the current belief in industrialized civiliza-
tions, such as that to be found in Great Britain, that the
purpose of life and the most valuable activity therein is
work, for the doing of which the doer gets paid. In assessing this valuation of the diversity of human life, we can

look both back and forward. Behind us, we have the aristocracy, the gentry and the clergy who held a different view: that mercenary work might be a necessary duty but that the more valuable things were done when economic compulsion was removed. Looking ahead into the more sophisticated future which science will inevitably bring about, what are now dubbed 'leisure activities' will occupy an increasing proportion of people's time and will, therefore, acquire higher prestige. Some activities which we now feel to be trivial and frivolous may then come to be recognized as acceptable and, indeed, good ways for a man or woman to fill his or her time at any age. In today's basically serious-minded social atmosphere 'games theory' is applied to business. In a more leisured age, it will seem legitimate to apply it also to games.

There are those for whom the aging process takes place more slowly than it does for the generality of people, and there are those who are endowed, both when they are young and when they are old, with more vigour, talent and enterprise than their fellows. These are the Bertrand Russells and the Marshal Titos, the Arthur Askeys and the Marlene Dietrichs, who continue to perform in their seventies and eighties, each in his or her particular sphere, when most of their contemporaries have come to a standstill. For the rest, there is much that can be done, partly by the application of scientific knowledge to maintain the physical well-being of the elderly and partly by the elderly themselves when they fully recognize their own value and capacity within the community, to postpone their slowdown and standstill to their appropriate times. Nevertheless, there is need for proper and wise provisions to be made for dealing with elderly people at the stage in their lives when their physical capacities are deteriorating.

A great deal has been done to help the elderly in their homes. Although it has been fashionable to criticize the provision of public welfare and to abuse the 'welfare state': the complex web of home helpers, 'meals on wheels' and trained social workers which covers the United Kingdom, it is, in its way, a remarkable testimony to socialized kindliness. The time may come, however, when it is best for some elderly people, when they are no longer able to manage their own affairs in their own home, to move into other accommodation. The reason may not lie in any exceptional deterioration in their own capacity; the problem may equally arise from the change in the social organization of the community, whereby the family has not only become fewer in numbers but, of that reduced number, everyone – the daughter, the wife, the aunt next door as well as the husband – find it necessary to go out of the house each day to travel somewhere else to work.

Following the stage wherein the elderly couple can satisfactorily live together, possibly with the support of a home helper provided by the community, there comes the next phase when, after the death of one of the partners (more often the husband) the one who is left needs further support. For those who can command some financial means, there are schemes such as the Abbeyfield Association. In a communally-owned house, each inmate has his or her own room where he or she can continue to live much as before, either pursuing a 'useful' activity or passing the time – as so many of us tend to do – with the day's little doings. For a comparatively modest rent, there are provided meals and warmth and a measure of surveillance.

The State, too, provides residential care for the elderly. In 1979 in a report of what was available in London, the Department of Health and Social Security pointed out that although much was done, the way it was done was variable. The houses used, as would be expected, were of diverse ages, sizes and degrees of suitability. And, as is found in a family environment, some of them were happier places than others. Whether elderly people – again like their younger fellow citizens – are all anxious to sit on advisory committees and be called upon constantly to express an opinion on matters where, in the received orthodoxy of modern 'participation', they are expected to exercise democratic rights, or whether they would rather rely on a good organizer to run the home for them, is a matter for debate. The degree to which they are consulted varies widely from one establishment to another. What really decides, however, whether the elderly people for whom the arrangements are made are able to live a satisfactory life is not so much whether they have appropriate meals, medical advice or nursing, but whether or not they are provided with too much. With all their needs taken care of, their shopping, the cleaning of their rooms and the cooking of their meals, the handling of their money and the maintenance of their television sets, nothing remains to be done except to sit and wait for the days to pass by. It is now being recognized that properly run homes, while exercising the appropriate technical supervision over their elderly occupants, must at the same time ensure that these residents retain a due measure of their independence. If this is really going to be achieved, they must be free to make mistakes and to take risks if they so wish. Those in charge must somehow make sure that they do not get themselves into unduly dangerous situations while at the same time allowing them to enjoy the same measure of danger they would meet as a grandmother or a grandfather in a reasonable household. There is a need to balance the degree of harm they are likely to get themselves into against the damage that will be done to their self-respect and independence if they are protectively prevented from ever running any risk at all.

It is perhaps humiliating for those who have made a specialist study of all that is new in scientific gerontology to find that one of the most successful arrangements for the management of the elderly in England was set up nearly three hundred and fifty years ago. This was the Royal Hospital in London. Charles II established the hospital – that is, the asylum for old soldiers. The Chelsea Pensioners, as they are called, are housed in a beautiful building in which each has a sleeping alcove where, if he wishes, he can be private. Each alcove opens onto the main common room, which is warmed – originally by coal fires – so that the sleeping quarters are warm too. The old pensioners are issued with an elegant scarlet uniform. From time to time they are engaged in ceremonial duties so that their self-respect is maintained and their memories of times past in the army kept fresh. They retain a portion of their pension so that, if they wish, they can visit, in all the dignity of their status, a nearby public house. It is true that it sometimes happens that motorists, driving along the Chelsea Bridge Road nearby, get a fright when a dignified old Pensioner, resplendent in his scarlet greatcoat, steps into the traffic without warning. After two or three near misses, an aging Pensioner may be forbidden to walk out alone, but beyond such exercises in sensible prudence, the traditional policy is to allow the Pensioners in their old age all the freedom they can handle. The Commandant told me of only one inmate whom it was found necessary to discharge. He was asked to leave when he became, at the age of seventy-five, engaged to be married.

There are nowadays old people's homes where this kind of approach is being combined with application of advanced scientific treatment. On the one hand, detailed investigation and active treatment are undertaken to diagnose and correct such disabilities as deafness, diabetes or failure of memory and, on the other hand, efforts are made to avoid such potentially harmful administrative deficiencies as a shortage of clothing, making it necessary to deprive elderly people of underclothes on a Sunday or, through what is perhaps merely a lack of imagination, putting residents to bed at nine o'clock in the evening, sometimes with a sedative if, as is likely, they are unable to sleep until morning. In other places, (there is one example in Buckinghamshire), those in charge of elderly residents arrange for young women to make regular visits and bring their children with them. This is a variant of another idea to arrange for young families who are kindly disposed to 'rent a granny'. The underlying principle is that the elderly people shall retain, not only their physical health, with heart, lungs, brain and joints functioning properly, but also their social well-being. It is as much a part of health to maintain some function within the community as for the various organs to function harmoniously within the body. While it is better if such social functioning extends outside the home in which they live, it is recognized as being important, too, that within the home people can get up and go to bed when they like, make themselves cups of tea if they choose, and so maintain as vigorous, diverse and satisfying a degree of social health as of physical health.

Death and the thought of death

Death which, regardless of what science may achieve, is the end of old age, has been neglected for much of the period during which the great advances in the understanding of the biological process of aging have been made. Scientific researchers have been so completely wrapped up in their efforts not only to comprehend what was happening but to postpone the inevitable termination of events, that they have given themselves little time to reflect on how death should best be faced. Indeed, the accusation has been made that medical scientists have been so deeply preoccupied in their efforts to prevent death occurring that it would almost seem as if they were prepared to assume that one day they might find a way to postpone it indefinitely. It has even been claimed that deep down in their minds they feel that the death of a patient is a sign of failure, a reproach to the scientist and consequently – like defeat in a boxing match – something which ought not to be contemplated.

Even though the old people themselves can be confident that the technical capacity of modern science is sufficient to ensure that their approaching dissolution will be painless, the lack of study and consideration for their latter end, and even the very fact that they will be made unconscious of the actual event, leaves them in an unsatisfied state. Regardless of the professional cheerfulness of those whose business it is to deal with the disabilities of advanced old age, death casts its shadow and, as they grow older, more people than many of those who attend on them would be prepared to admit can see it approaching.

Comparatively recently, a number of geriatricians have become aware that the employment of scientific means to maintain the functioning of the body beyond the point at which the integrity of the man or woman as a person can be expected to survive is wrong. At this point, most of the pharmacological and technical processes by which one or other of the failing systems of the body have been supported are continued no longer and the patient is transferred to a hospital for the dying. While this arrangement may be accepted by elderly people as a seemly avenue through which to terminate their life span, further study may show that, for the future, there could be worked out a better and more carefully considered arrangement for this, the last and, as once was thought, the most important phase of life.

One of the most thoughtful and also one of the most scholarly studies of what the final phase of old age and the end of the life of a man or woman involves was that carried out within the new discipline of behavioural science by Phillipe Aries.* Aries has collated evidence to

* *Western Attitudes Towards Death*, P. Aries, Johns Hopkins
University Press (Baltimore), 1974.

show that Western attitudes to death have over the centuries passed through a number of stages. Although, as a scientist, he makes no judgment but merely assembles his evidence, this evidence has lessons for our modern technological age. To start with, he points out that in the millenium ending in about the twelfth century, men and women had come to terms with death. They knew that it was a part of life and faced with equanimity the thought that they would one day die. We do not do so in this modern scientific age. Indeed, so repugnant is the idea of dying that the latter end of life is disturbed by our pathetic pretence that death will never occur. In those early days, people knew when they were about to die. They could face the fact that they had come to their death bed. The old man would call his sons about him and tell them 'my death is near'. Death, although it was recognized as inevitable, had been tamed. This spirit of certainty – of dignity, if you will – continued among a minority of great men and women long after the general vulgar attitude had changed. On 29 July 1750, the day of his death, Johann Sebastian Bach, as is described by Anna Magdalena Bach, behaved as '. . . feeling his end approach'. Tolstoy, too, lying sick in a rural railway station, knew that he was going to die.

Those who faced death in this way, knowing that they were at death's door, could prepare themselves for the event. They could themselves arrange the seemly ritual, over which they, and they alone, presided. They had become familiar with what they would have to do through having attended death-bed scenes before. Yet familiarity did not trivialize the ritual. The bodies of the dead were treated with respect (not left in cold storage pending the resolution of an industrial dispute) and sent out of the city into the custody of the church.

During the second half of the Middle Ages from, say, the eleventh or twelfth centuries, a subtle modification took place in people's attitude to death. They were still

familar with death and accepted it – as we do not today –
and accepted it, too, with the proper amount of due solemnity, as one of the frontier posts through which each
generation had to pass. But two important new ingredients had come to be introduced. The first was the idea
of judgment. A man's life was not unimportant, as ours
so often seems to be today in our crowded computerized
world, but something that was to be judged as good or
evil. Secondly, there was the notion that how a man
comported himself on the Day of Judgment, as his whole
life flashed before his eyes, was important too. Even in
death, a person still had significant and worthwhile
things to do. From the end of the Middle Ages until virtually half-way through the nineteenth century, before
the idea of man's secular control of now and hereafter
through the cleverness of his science diminished the
heavens and the earth, the ritual solemnity of the death-
bed persisted. The dying man had a central role to play
in the ceremonies surrounding his own death. He was at
the centre of events, presiding over the occasion and
determining the character of an important ritual as he
saw fit.

It would be wrong to suggest that there were many
people who looked forward to their own death with
pleasure. This was not so. But in those earlier pre-
scientific times, before the taboo which prevented even
the mention of death, the last days of old age could be
made more equable and the dignity and value of life
retained to the end by the courageous anticipation of a
good death.

The men of the Middle Ages, however, also possessed
an acuter love of life and its possessions than we do now.
In reflecting on their deaths, the people of those times
wept that they would have to leave behind them their
houses and their orchards, the rich clothes and beautiful
ornaments which they had collected during their lifetime. This sadness and the delight in our *temperalia* we

have lost today. The geriatric patient, alone in bed in a hospital gown which opens all the way down the back, has already been deprived of his possessions.

Aries puts forward evidence to suggest that our attitude to death began to change in the second half of the eighteenth century. Note the radio SOS messages when a separated son is summoned not to his father's death-bed, but to such-and-such a hospital where his father is 'dangerously ill'. When ultimately there is no alternative but to recognize the imminence of death, we all – ourselves the dying, our relatives, workmates, and the doctors – feel that the whole business is disappointing and unsatisfactory. It was in the eighteenth century that people gave up facing their own death. Before then, as a man lay dying he gave orders to a son, 'look after your mother', to two brothers, 'stop quarrelling and live in peace with one another'. A man's will was more than a document disposing of his property. It was a series of pious instructions from the one who was about to die to his successor. Then, as the modern age began to dawn, the idea of an old man being responsible for his own behaviour and in a position to instruct those whom he was leaving behind was abandoned. The elderly gave up their seniority and abdicated. The family were then in charge, soon to be followed by the anonymous governors of the nationalized hospital. The will (the word is indeed evocative) of the dying man has become no more than a piece of paper transferring property to the possession of a legatee.

Why is it that in the middle of the twentieth century, death, so omnipresent in the past as to be familiar, its approach an integral part of life and, for the fortunate, the final phase of old age, should have become shameful and forbidden? The answer, perhaps, lies in the gradual growth of the assumption that, through our own cleverness, science could do anything. It therefore became accepted that the very presence of death in the midst of

happy life was a disturbance which, if it could not actually be avoided altogether, should at least not be mentioned. The function of science was to ensure that life
should always be comfortable, warm, well lit and – in
short – happy. Not only should the fact that elderly people were going to die be kept from them, but it should
not be admitted – at least, until the last moment – by
anyone else. Furthermore, the technicalities of so-called
'intensive care' had become so complex that it was generally accepted that the site of death should be moved.
One could no longer expect to die at home, where one
had standing as the principal inhabitant and the defer-
ence and affection of one's family, but in a busy hospital,
alone, among strangers. These busy strangers, each one
trained to perform his or her appropriate 'industrial
action', were in a false position too. Hospitals have long
lost their function as shelters for the poor and have
become medical centres where those with knowledge
and the appropriate apparatus heal the sick and join in a
battle against death which, in accordance with the
demands of their scientific training they must always
assume that they have a good chance of winning.

There are today a number of newer hospitals – if this
is the right word – where the dying are recognized as
such and are kindly treated. Even so, the activity is all on
the side of the attendants. No initiative remains with the
inmates. They are there because it is inconvenient for
them to die at home. The initiative has passed from the
dying person, first – at some time in the eighteenth century – to the family and now, in our own time, to the
doctor and the hospital team. These are experts whose
purpose is to obtain for their patients 'an acceptable
style' of dying. This acceptability is something that will
not embarrass the smooth life-style of modern secular
existence. The highest exaltation which can now be
promised for the elderly person at the end of his or her
life – the culminating pinnacle of all those years of living – is to die unconscious.

Not being able to abolish death, the modern citizen tries to pretend that it does not occur. The transfer from the hospital to the crematorium is carried out with the efficiency of an exercise in 'materials transfer' in a factory. Once at the crematorium, the body is made to disappear without trace. In the United States, the community which is at the forefront of technological civilization, the refusal to accept the reality of death has gone furthest of all. Medical technology enfolds the last hours of living more completely than anywhere else, and even when the pumps and valves, the electrical pulses and mechanical aerators are shut off and what was once a thinking, feeling, doubting creature dies, the dead body is embalmed, prepared and coloured to look as if it were still alive, and even dressed in a suit or costume to blend, just as if it were another mourner, with the rest of the people from the office who have come together for the brief, impersonal funeral ceremony. And people do not wish to be reminded either, that, once the ceremony is over, anything untoward – such as decay or putrefaction – is going to take place. The body, therefore, is put into a coffin guaranteed to remain water-resistant for a hundred years or, for those who are very rich, put into a deep-freeze cabinet so that it can at any time in the future be brought back to life when – as those who pay for the equipment believe, but oh so mistakenly – science discovers a way to abolish death and enable us to live for ever.

Thus have we changed the last days of old age. Thus has the status of the elderly in their final period of life diminished. And thus have we diminished ourselves, both when we are in the fullness of busy life and in our later days, by closing our eyes to the inevitability of death, to the dignity and purpose which it gives to life and, to use a thought once familar but now no longer current, to the understanding that a good death can be a proper complement to a good life.

The many advantages which the elderly living in this

present scientific age can enjoy have been brought into focus in the course of these reflections on old age. We can see that the later decades of life, which many of our ancestors never reached, are as fully available for proper and meaningful activity as any other phase of life. It is up to us to organize our society so as to make available to elderly people the opportunities which they can properly take and to make provision for the appropriate distribution to them of a fair share of the community's wealth. These things are being done, not perfectly perhaps, but with better understanding as time goes by.

Two aspects of the nation's approach to old age, however, need further attention and greater endeavour. Already scientific advances have brought rich rewards, in initial progress in research into dementia, in some amelioration of stroke, arthritis, circulatory and respiratory diseases. But the problems are not yet solved. In the light of what could be accomplished and of the increase in the numbers of the elderly within the community, there are too few research centres in the universities and hospitals of the country. This state of affairs needs to be remedied. In 1975, Professor Brocklehurst* was only able to enumerate in Great Britain seven university chairs in geriatric medicine in universities other than his own, and estimated the number of medical specialists in geriatrics at about six hundred and fifty. Those among the elderly who continue in good health and productive endeavour into their nineties indicate that diseases and disabilities of old age are no more an essential part of life than tuberculosis, smallpox and cholera, once the scourges of man's prime, are now seen to be.

The second change which the accounts of the diverse aspects of aging, as delineated in this book, show to be necessary is a change in attitude. I forbear to argue

---

* *Geriatric Care in Advanced Societies*, ed. J. C. Brocklehurst, MTB, 1975.

whether this same change in attitude would be of benefit to the whole community, old and young alike, but there seems to be no doubt that it is overdue for the elderly. The awakening, for which the present condition of the elderly cries out, is for an enhanced recognition of the value of the individual. The American crime of 'agism', recognized as discrimination in employment on account of age against people who wish to work and are capable of doing so, may represent an advance in our perception of the rights of the elderly. The idea, however, could be broadened to allow people who have worked an appropriate amount to have the opportunity of doing something else or of living a useful and seemly life devoted to activities other than those of economic endeavour, and receiving appropriate esteem as worthy citizens and valuable men and women while doing so.

A caring society in which there is provision of health care, of adequate financial support and appropriate food and shelter, such as it is the purpose of our present society to provide, is praiseworthy. When we attach an equal value to the dignity of every citizen, young as well as old, and each citizen comes to recognize his own value, then indeed will the expectations for old people be seen to have progressed towards fulfilment.

Index